A Call to Holy Living

A Call to Holy Living

WALKING WITH GOD
IN JOY, PRAISE, AND
GRATITUDE

Bruce Larson

AUGSBURG Publishing House • Minneapolis

A CALL TO HOLY LIVING
Walking with God in Joy, Praise, and Gratitude

Copyright © 1988 Augsburg Publishing House

Scripture quotations unless otherwise noted are from the Holy Bible: New International Version. Copyright 1978 by the New York International Bible Society. Used by permission of Zondervan Bible Publishers.

Scripture quotations marked TEV are from The Good News Bible, Today's English Version, copyright 1966, 1971, 1976 by American Bible Society. Used by permission.

Library of Congress Cataloging-in-Publication Data

Larson, Bruce.
    A call to holy living: walking with God in joy, praise, and
gratitude / Bruce Larson.
      p.   cm.
    ISBN 0-8066-2305-5
    1. Spiritual life—Presbyterian authors. I. Title.
BV4501.2.L3195 1988
248.4—dc19

    87-34579
    CIP

Manufactured in the U.S.A.   APH 10-0963

1 2 3 4 5 6 7 8 9 0 1 2 3 4 5 6 7 8 9

Contents

Editor's Foreword   9
Preface   11

 1   *The Design for Holy Living*   15
 2   *A Call to Faith*   27
 3   *Terms of the Call*   34
 4   *A Call to Peace and a Call to War*   44
 5   *Great Expectations*   54
 6   *The Touch of Love*   63
 7   *At the Heart of Holy Living*   71
 8   *A Call to Rejoice*   78
 9   *Dialog: Jesus Prays for Us*   86
10   *Dialog: What, Where, and Why*   97
11   *A Peacemaker's Dialog*   107
12   *Dangerous Dialog*   117

Editor's Foreword

Christian life—like all life—is dynamic. It has direction and involves growth. "Instead, by speaking the truth in a spirit of love, we must grow up in every way to Christ, who is the head" (Eph. 4:15 TEV). God *calls* us to grow. "Grow in the grace and knowledge of our Lord and Savior Jesus Christ" (2 Peter 3:18). We grow in what God has given us— the grace of being in a relationship with him.

Christian growth is both personal and corporate. Living in interdependence with others, we grow within the Christian community—the body of Christ. This growth is the work of the Holy Spirit. Paul spelled it out clearly: "The fruit of the Spirit is love, joy, peace, patience, kindness, goodness, faithfulness, gentleness and self-control" (Gal. 5:22).

Although the analogy is from nature's growth from blossom to fruit, Christian growth is not completed in our lifetime. We are always moving, but never arriving. Actually we grow in our *awareness* of our need for growth. And Christian growth may not be as observable to the senses as is nature's fruit. It is patterned after the crucifixion and resurrection of Christ. The experience is seldom steady and gradual. The way *up* may be the way *down*. The new comes out of the death of the old.

Christian growth is therefore a venture of faith that focuses on forgiveness. It happens in response to God's call and is secured only by God's grace.

God calls us to grow by creating within us a desire for it. "As a deer longs for a stream of cool water, so I long for you, O God" (Ps. 42:1 TEV). Peter also described this desire: "Crave pure spiritual milk, so that by it you may grow up in your salvation, now that you have tasted that the Lord is good" (1 Peter 2:2). Jesus described it as "hungering and thirsting." "Blessed are those who hunger and thirst for righteousness, for they will be filled" (Matt. 5:6).

The books in this series are intended as helps in this pilgrimage of growth. Each one deals with a particular facet of this adventure. Growth takes place in interaction with the human community. It involves not only our relationship with God but also our relationships with people. In this book, a well-known and respected spiritual guide presents Christian growth as our response to God's call to holy living. Using his rich resource of experience, Bruce Larson describes, in very practical terms, how our faith can influence our lives.

The guidelines for holy living are in the Bible. Larson focuses on these guidelines from the letter to the Ephesians in the first part of the book, the letter to the Philippians in the middle part, and from the Gospels—with the emphasis on Jesus' modeling and teaching regarding *prayer*—in the last part.

The author shares himself freely with his readers and is generous with illustrations. He has provided us with a positive-minded, spiritually oriented, and Christ-centered guide for living the kind of life that befits our calling. By concluding with prayer, he has highlighted this inner dialog as the beginning and the end of holy living.

WILLIAM E. HULME

Preface

One of the clear, unifying, central messages of the Bible is God's invitation—even more, God's imperative—to all humankind to lead a holy life. This is a message reiterated throughout the Old and New Testaments, from Genesis through Revelation.

To be *holy* means to be "set apart" for the purpose the Lord had in mind when he made us. Certainly we are set apart to serve God. But, just as important, in the words of the *Westminster Catechism*, we are "to glorify God and to enjoy Him forever." The holy living we are called to has nothing to do with piety or spiritual posturing. It is, however, a life of purpose, obedience, and joy.

The vitality of the church in every age depends on those who hear and affirm God's call to holy living and who make that pursuit the principal agenda for their lives, whether they achieve it or not. In the last half of the 20th century Christians have largely been divided about the definition of that call. We are polarized between those who interpret holy living to mean the radical reshaping of this present world and those for whom holy living means a personal relationship with a living God that radicalizes the inner landscape of one's soul, mind, and spirit.

Of course, both of these groups, which rarely speak to each other, are right—and both are wrong. *Heresy* can be defined as a partial truth that is held to the exclusion of the whole truth. In recent years we have witnessed the powerful emergence on the political scene of that part of the "personalist" group called "fundamentalists." Whether or not one agrees with the views of the Moral Majority and similar organizations, they are attempting to redefine the call to holy living so that it includes political and social responsibilities, and that is a cause for rejoicing. It would be equally encouraging if the socially and politically concerned part of the family of faith would begin to expand *its* focus to include the need for a personal experience of God and an active devotional life.

This book is an attempt to reinforce the biblical mandate to view life as a whole and to explore the ensuing social and political implications of that view. Two of my favorite New Testament books, Ephesians and Philippians, will provide the basis for these reflections. Paul's letter to the Philippians unashamedly celebrates the personal dimensions of our call, while Ephesians gives us a breathtaking view of the universal relevance and cosmic dimensions of Jesus Christ.

The final third of this book deals, as it must, with prayer. The Bible is our only record of what God *has* said and done with his people in the past. Prayer, on the other hand, is dialog with the living God who is speaking *now* and acting still. It is in the arena of prayer that God is able to speak a fresh, new, never-before-heard word. We speak to God about our needs and the needs of our neighbors and the world. As we listen in prayer, God speaks to us about his current strategy for supplying those needs. God motivates us to be his peacemakers and ministers in a terrifying and desperate world. The other side of prayer is that God is praying for us to be the answer to his hopes for the world, even as we pray for God to meet our needs and hopes.

Philippians and Ephesians are immutable guidelines for the holy living to which God calls us. They are like bookends embracing the full gamut of that call from personal obedience and inner joy to political relevance. We Christians may or may not feel holy most of the time, but it is only in the pursuit of holy living that we are wholly living.

I believe deeply in the message of this book, which originates entirely with God's written Word. But there would be no *Call to Holy Living* without the editorial skills of my wife, Hazel Marie. Once again, she has taken a group of sermons preached to the faithful and exciting saints at University Presbyterian Church and made them into a book. I trust God will speak to you through these pages and enable you to hear and respond to his call to holy living.

BRUCE LARSON
Seattle, Washington

1

The Design
for Holy Living

Recently I received a highly complimentary letter in the mail. The writer claimed I was a valued person, one of a very select group of individuals chosen to receive an opportunity not extended to the average citizen. Furthermore, I was successful, self-confident, one whose life-style requires special privileges. The bottom line was this: by sending in $65, I could have an American Express Gold Card. These affirmations came from no less an authority than Mr. John Sutphin, Senior Vice President for American Express.

We've all received enough mail like that to know that we cannot take these evaluations of our importance too seriously. Our success or lack of it needs to be defined much more personally and specifically. We Christians measure our success or failure against different criteria. The Scriptures provide a clear message of who we are as God's people, what we are to do, and how we are to live. And perhaps there is no place where that message is more clearly laid out for us than in Paul's letter to the Ephesians.

Someone has said we are quick to believe the incredible, while remaining skeptical about the everyday. Told that there are three hundred billion stars in the universe, we say, "Of course." On the other hand, a simple sign saying "Wet Paint" tempts us to test its truth. I think the book of Ephesians invites us to make that kind of see-for-yourself test. Coleridge, the English poet, called Ephesians the most profound book in existence. Others have claimed that it is the most divine composition ever written. Known as the "queen of the Epistles," it stands alone as an overview—from God's perspective—of God's master plan for creation, for the church, and for us personally.

Though the authorship of Ephesians is not entirely verifiable, it is generally credited to the apostle Paul. At the time it was written, between A.D. 60 and 63, Paul was in prison at Rome and very likely awaiting his execution. It was probably not addressed to the Ephesians only. There are no references to the particular saints at Ephesus. It lacks Paul's usual relational style, the personal touch so evident in other letters: "Give my greetings to the brothers at Laodicia and to Nympha . . . ," "Tell Archapus . . . ," "Greet Priscilla and Aquilla. . . ." We can assume it was written as a circular letter to a number of churches. It is a magnificent theological treatise—one of Paul's last legacies to Christendom.

Also unlike other Pauline epistles, the letter does not address one specific problem. If anything, Paul wrote in order to broaden the horizons of those infant Christian churches. He wanted them to understand, from God's perspective, that to which they had been called. He was alarmed by the political and ethical divisions in the early church, and we still have such divisions in the church today. There was recurring conflict between the Jewish Christians and the

Gentile Christians. Those who were formerly Jews kept most of their old forms—circumcision and the strict observance of the Sabbath and of dietary laws. The Gentile Christians refused to adopt those rules and regulations, insisting that the new covenant in Christ rendered the old Jewish laws and customs unnecessary.

In addressing this major division in the household of faith, Paul made it clear that there is liberty and freedom in Jesus Christ, but also emphasized the universality and the unity made possible in him. Throughout the epistle, the key word is *one*. We are one; the Father is one with us; we are one with one another. Together, we make up one body with one. Lord, one faith, one Baptism.

Sir Thomas Beecham, the eminent conductor of the London Symphony, often acted as guest conductor for other orchestras. On one occasion he was having a good deal of difficulty with a seemingly undisciplined group of musicians. During rehearsal he was asked by the concertmaster how he wanted a particular section played. After a long pause and with great forbearance, he replied, "Together." That's what Paul was saying here—that individual Christian believers are called to do and be something together—to be, in fact, one.

Actually, Paul was attempting to lay out for those early church members God's master plan. In the first chapter he wrote, "And he made known to us the mystery of his will according to his good pleasure, which he purposed in Christ, to be put into effect when the times will have reached their fulfillment—to bring all things in heaven and on earth together under one head, even Christ" (Eph. 1:9-10). Paul proclaimed the centrality of Jesus Christ for all of life—the present and the future, in heaven and on earth.

Someone once asked the noted theologian Karl Barth

what he considered the most profound theological statement
he had ever read. His answer was, "Jesus loves me, this I
know, for the Bible tells me so." Those lines may very well
sum up all we need to know, but behind that simple truth
is God's master plan for all things. And if we are unaware
of that grand design, we can get lost on the faith journey.
We may be like the guide who was hired by some hunters
to take them into the backwoods of Maine. After some days,
they became hopelessly lost and quite naturally began to
doubt the competence of their guide. "You said you were
the best guide in Maine," they reminded him. "I am," he
said, "but I think we're in Canada now." Theologically
speaking, we can wander forever in a foreign land unless
we understand the master design of our Creator, who, speaking through Paul, laid out his plans and purposes for the
church.

There are three major parts to that grand design that are
described in the very first chapter of Ephesians, beginning
with verse 3: "Praise be to the God and Father of our Lord
Jesus Christ, who has blessed us in the heavenly realms with
every spiritual blessing in Christ. For he chose us in him
before the creation of the world to be holy and blameless
in his sight." Part one of the plan is that we are *chosen* by
God from the beginning of the world.

Part two of the plan is described beginning with verse 5:
"In love he predestined us to be adopted as his sons through
Jesus Christ, in accordance with his pleasure and will. . . .
In him we have redemption through his blood, the forgive-
ness of sins, in accordance with the riches of God's grace
that he lavished on us with all wisdom and understanding."
Having been chosen by the Father then, we are *redeemed*
by the Son.

Further on, in verse 13, we read, "And you also were

included in Christ when you heard the word of truth, the gospel of your salvation. Having believed, you were marked in him with a seal, the promised Holy Spirit, who is a deposit guaranteeing our inheritance until the redemption of those who are God's possession—to the praise of his glory." That is the third dimension of the master plan. We are *sealed* by the Holy Spirit.

I am partial to the King James translation of verse 14, where the phrase "a deposit guaranteeing our inheritance" is "the earnest of our inheritance." If you have ever purchased any real estate, you're familiar with the concept of "earnest money." It is an amount you give the seller to prove good faith and to demonstrate that you are in earnest. It is a guarantee that the whole amount will be forthcoming later on. Imagine! The indwelling Holy Spirit with all his accompanying gifts and fruits is only the down payment for all that God has in mind to give us.

The apostle Paul tells us, then, that we are chosen by the Father, redeemed by the Son, and sealed by the guarantee of the Spirit. But to what end? God's purposes for us are outlined in the last two verses of Chapter 1: "And God placed all things under his feet and appointed him to be head over everything for the church, which is his body . . ." (1:22-23). Christ is the center, the head of all things, and you and I make up his body. It is God's plan that the church be the unifying force for *everything* in the world. It is a mind-boggling mandate, and one we need to take more seriously.

The universities founded in the Middle Ages were constructed with a chapel at the center. Theology was considered the queen of the sciences. The architecture of the time confirmed the prevailing belief that understanding the revelation of God in Jesus Christ was the beginning of all learning. Around that central focus were the buildings for mathematics, astronomy, geometry, and music. All the other disciplines were to revolve around the centrality of God as revealed in Jesus Christ. In our own time, I believe we are experiencing a new awareness of the preeminence of Christ and his lordship in all sorts of unexpected areas and disciplines. We are starting to explore the implications and applications of the gospel for all of secular society.

The church—meaning the body of believers—is the unifying force for much that is new in medicine. Pioneers in wholistic medicine understand what Jesus has said and is still saying about the spiritual nature of wellness and wholeness. Key words in medicine now are *hope, faith,* and *love.* Illness, we are told, is brought on by loneliness, stress, and destructive life-styles. These are all nonmedical terms, and they reflect a new understanding of our spiritual nature.

There are some areas in which it is especially difficult to believe the church can be a unifying force. Certainly economics, that hard-nosed science, is one of them. Yet a Christian group called Habitat for Humanity is in the forefront of that kind of endeavor. All over the world they are building homes for poor people through volunteer labor and interest-free loans. And I think we are all coming to a new appreciation of what a biblical approach to economics might mean. Falling oil prices have resulted in our nation's inability to collect the huge debts owed us by other nations. If we are to survive as a global family, we need to rethink our economic policies as they affect our brothers and sisters worldwide, both inside and outside the household of faith.

No less an authority than the former chief justice of the Supreme Court, Warren Burger, has said that our society's emphasis on litigation is destroying us. If that is to be corrected, we need more and more to discover forgiveness, reconciliation, and peacemaking. The church of Jesus Christ is the one place where those attitudes are pursued and emphasized. In Seattle, where I live, the Christian Conciliation Service of Puget Sound has been formed to offer Christians a viable alternative to the present dead-end court system.

In this decade we are also seeing a new direction in the business world. The key to success in business seems to be happy employer-employee relationships. The Japanese were the first to understand that important dimension. Their manufacturing firms operate as families. I read recently that Gortex, a firm making waterproof fabric, is trying a new approach to call forth the creativity in workers and develop a family atmosphere. Every employee has the title of vice-president and is given the opportunity to move around the various departments to determine where he or she can best operate. It seems to me that even these small advances are attempts to put into practice the unity and harmony that Paul is exhorting us to in Ephesians.

A local police captain called on me recently. One of his goals for the force is that they might learn to *proact* to problems, rather than *react*—to deal with problems as they are forming and not just to solve them after they have happened. We discussed a particular case involving a young orphan raised by unloving relatives who consequently got into enough trouble with the law to be sent off to the penitentiary while still a teenager. He returned a hardened criminal. Society's outcry is, "Why didn't they rehabilitate him?" Who exactly are *they?* The tragedy is that an institution as such cannot rehabilitate anyone. That should have been attempted much earlier on by the community and by the church. As we love and befriend a troubled youngster, we are making a positive impact, however small, in the field of law enforcement.

The church has the potential to be a unifying force for nations at enmity all over the globe. Experts in Middle East politics have told me that apart from a spiritual awakening, there is no hope that there will ever be peace in that area. Both Israel and the neighboring Islamic countries tend to operate out of the principle of revenge—"an eye for an eye and a tooth for a tooth." Wrongs are to be avenged, however long it takes. Land lost generations ago is still fiercely contended for. How can these two groups ever live together and forgive each other unless they discover a God who bids them to forgive their enemies? I believe that the only hope for peace in the Middle East, or anywhere else, is in the lordship of Jesus Christ.

God's dreams for us, as they are detailed by Paul in Ephesians, speak of both a new society and a new humanity. And a new kind of person is to be a part of that new order. Chapter 2 includes these words: "God, who is rich in mercy, made us alive with Christ even when we were dead in transgressions" (vv. 4-5). This new humanity will have new life. In John 10:10 Jesus said, "I have come that they may have life, and have it to the full." The Greek word used for "life" is *zoe*, which means life pressed down, heaped up, and running over. That new kind of life was anticipated in the Old Testament. Ezekiel 36:26 says, "I will give you a new heart and put a new spirit in you; I will remove from you your heart of stone and give you a heart of flesh." That new heart and new spirit enables us to be peacemakers, reconcilers, forgivers, lovers, and builders of community, and to envision this world as one people under the lordship of the one who is both Creator and Redeemer.

This second chapter of Paul's letter outlines the new humanity, and it would seem to develop in three phases: what we *were*, what we *are*, and what we *will be*. I once heard a very rustic new Christian give his witness in this way: "I ain't what I want to be and I ain't what I'm gonna be, but I thank God I ain't what I was." We can all say that because even though we are far from perfect, God has put a new spirit into us. God has taken that old heart of stone—unforgiving, unbending, unyielding, critical, and judgmental—and changed it so that we are able to reach out to the undeserving, the unlovely, the unwashed, the unrewarding. We care because we are cared for. That's what it means to be the new creation.

Carl Jung, colleague of Freud and pioneer psychoanalyst, was deeply spiritual and he believed in God. At the end of his long and successful career he is reported to have said, "Among all my patients over 35, there has not been one whose problem in the last resort was not that of finding a religious outlook on life." God is the integrating factor of your personality and mine. God is the center for all of life.

The 1985 movie *The Color Purple* was a stunning drama about one black woman's struggle for survival, dignity, and personhood in a brutalizing environment. The first hour was so horrifying that my wife kept threatening to leave the theater. But in the second hour you began to see the triumph of the human spirit and the triumph of God's grace. At one point one of the main characters, who has been beaten and unjustly imprisoned, turns to Celia, the heroine, and says, "When you came into that store, I knew there was a God." You and I, as members of Christ's body, have that power. We can go into a courtroom, a school, an office, or a neighborhood as walking demonstrations of the new humanity.

Paul goes on in Chapter 2 to speak about our unity and where it comes from. He pleads with the Jewish and Gentile Christians to be one. In verses 8 and 9 we read, "For it is by grace you have been saved, through faith—and this not from yourselves, it is the gift of God—not by works, so that no one can boast." Verse 13 underscores that: "But now in

Christ Jesus you who once were far away have been brought near through the blood of Christ."

How much we in the church still struggle with this matter of unity! One of our pastoral staff members at University Presbyterian had the audacity to give the rest of us the Myers-Briggs Test. The main thing we discovered was what a hopelessly diverse group we are. Some of us are intuitive and some of us are logical. Some of us are compulsively organized and some of us are free spirits. We are certainly not all one personality type—all of which is to the glory of God.

The divisions within our congregation are just as vast, on issues both serious and not so serious. There are those who insist on formalism and those who press for spontaneity in worship. Jess Moody, pastor of the First Baptist Church in Van Nuys, California, has said, "I'd rather fry in fanaticism than freeze in formalism." I don't want to have to make that choice, if I can avoid it. I'm for the formalists and I'm for the freewheelers. We have a group of traditionalists who love the old music—and I agree it's hard, if not impossible, to improve on Bach, Beethoven, Handel, or Mozart. On the other hand, there are those innovators who want new songs that express God's love in a new way. Both have a valid point of view.

Every meeting of our congregation's elders is a confrontation between the cautious and the bold. The cautious say, "We're not meeting our budget. Let's cut back." The bold say, "Not meeting our budget? Let's raise more money." Between the two, we learn to distinguish between faith and responsibility. Every board has its task-oriented people who say, "We have a job to do for God. Let's get on with it." And they don't always seem concerned about how many bodies they step over to accomplish that. They are challenged by the process-oriented people, with their emphasis on relationships, who say, "Wait a minute. The job may never get done, but in the meantime, we're going to learn to love each other."

Then there are those long-standing opponents, the conservatives and the liberals. Someone has said that conservatives come to every meeting as though they had just come down from Mount Sinai with the Ten Commandments, while liberals stand at the bottom of the mountain with an eraser. How can those two groups live and worship together? Only by the gift of a new spirit. I don't know exactly how the blood of Jesus Christ reconciles and cleanses. Neither do I understand how water quenches our thirst, but it does. And Jesus Christ, by his life, death, and resurrection, is our hope for new life and a new humanity.

An old friend who had a great impact on my life died about 10 years ago. She was born in the lap of luxury. She actually grew up in New York's Waldorf-Astoria Hotel, the child of millionaire parents. Her life began to go awry just after her first marriage. She traveled with the wrong crowd, got hooked on drugs and alcohol and promiscuous sex, and finally divorced her husband. Her money, her health, and her luck all ran out and, in despair, she attempted suicide. At that point she phoned her former husband and told him her situation. "Wyn, I have nothing left." His response? "It's OK, Gert. I'll take care of it."

On that very day, enough money was deposited in her bank account to last her through the rest of her life. Her ex-husband was at that time president of Merrill-Lynch. The woman was Gert Behanna, lay evangelist and author of *The Late Liz,* who, some three miserable marriages later, found faith in Jesus Christ and became part of the new humanity that Paul describes for us in Ephesians.

Sometimes we come to the place where we say, "I can't go on, Father. I've run out of resources." And God says, "Don't worry. I'll take care of it." That's who God is and what a master plan he has for us. There's mercy and grace and forgiveness deposited to your account, enough to last through this life and eternity.

2

A Call
to Faith

The faith dilemma. It's an acute one for those of us in the last half of the 20th century. In whom and what shall we believe? Where shall we commit ourselves and our resources? The spectrum of possibilities seems inexhaustible, and encompasses both the ridiculous and the admirable.

Let's start with the ridiculous. You can join the Hari Krishnas and shave your head, wear a saffron robe, and tinkle finger bells and dance through the streets of your city. You can become a Moonie, selling flowers at airports, or exchanging wedding vows with hundreds of other brides and grooms in a mass service, arranged and performed by the Reverend Moon himself. Before the Rajneesh was forced out of Oregon, you could have joined those childish disciples of hedonism in a special community there. Their faith is not cluttered up with ideas about God or religion. You simply follow the Guru. Then there are the more respectable bidders for your faith—the Jehovah's Witnesses, those tireless door-to-door evangelists; the Mormons, models of civic pride and respectability; and the quiet and solid Christian Scientists. Secular causes and disciplines are also in the bidding, from communism and secular humanism to less widespread ideologies such as EST, Scientology, or astrology.

Then there is the Christian camp. Here again there is a spectrum, a variety of voices each telling us, "This is the way," and that way may be either narrow or broad, depending on the spokesman. You may be a disciple of Bill Gothard and attend his week-long workshops and sit for days and days filling notebooks on exactly how to live your life, how to behave, and what to believe. At the other extreme is someone like the head of our local Council of Churches, who said in a recent article, "I'm a Christian. I try to model my life on Jesus and to help people be all they can be." His faith is general and unspecific. Inclusion is paramount. Orthodoxy is secondary and negotiable.

There is just as much disagreement about the Christian faith among the clergy. One of England's bishops has said, "The clergy in my diocese—some are going out of their minds, some have already gone out of their minds, and some have no minds to go out of." There is no monolithic group known as "the clergy." Belief and practice differ enormously within that profession.

It might be helpful for us to consider exactly where it is that Christians are to invest their faith. Where is yours invested? It may be in doctrines and creeds. You've read and studied and learned and have a sense of certainty about what Scripture says about God's nature and about the meaning of life. Or, your faith may rest in personal ethics. The Scriptures have given you clear guidelines on how to behave. Your own goodness is the center of your faith. And for some Christians, faith is linked to a particular brand of politics.

Inside the Christian camp we have all kinds of choices available, from the Moral Majority to the advocates of the

Sanctuary Movement. There's a wide choice of "proper" politics for the Christian. It's even more common to invest our faith in a particular church (usually the one to which we belong), or in our denomination. We may feel certain of our salvation because we are Catholic or Presbyterian, Baptist or Lutheran.

It is thrilling to realize that Baptism has, for two thousand years, been done in the name of the Father, the Son, and the Holy Spirit. You are baptized into the church universal, not into the Methodist church or the Roman Catholic church or any other branch of Christ's church. That's part of the mystery of the Christian faith.

In the third chapter of Ephesians, Paul challenges the church then and now to believe *less* but to believe it more passionately. In fact, we are called to bet our lives on that belief. Paul said he was called "to preach to the Gentiles the unsearchable riches of Christ" (3:8). That's the heart of our faith. Paul says here and throughout the New Testament that our faith had better be in a person. Ultimate truth is a person, not a creed or doctrine, not a tradition or a denomination, not ethical behavior or moral persuasion—no matter how worthwhile any of those things might be. Our faith had better be in the ultimate person—Jesus Christ.

We read in Isaiah 65:1 that God said, "I revealed myself to those who did not ask for me; I was found by those who did not seek me. To a nation that did not call on my name, I said, 'Here am I, here am I.'" God has been saying, "Here am I," throughout history. He said it to Abraham, to Isaac, to Jacob, and to all of the Old Testament prophets, until the mystery was revealed to all of us in Jesus Christ. The mystery hidden for ages, hinted at and promised through the Old Testament, was made manifest in Jesus.

Our faith is not in a God who acted only in the past, a God who simply created the universe, set it in motion, and now watches events dispassionately. Nor is our faith in a God who will act only in the future, who will some day come again and close the curtain on history. Our faith is rather in a God who, by the Holy Spirit, comes in the present tense and says, as he did in Isaiah, "Here am I." We may feel more uncomfortable trusting God with the past or the future, but he is asking us to trust him with the now, to bet our lives on who he is and what he can do.

Let's say that someone has said or might someday say to you, "I love you. Will you marry me?" You can't simply respond by saying, "True. I believe in marriage." That is not an appropriate response to a person. You can say, "Yes, I will," or you can say, "No, I'm sorry. I cannot marry you." The unity that Paul speaks of all through Ephesians is the unity that results from committing our lives to and trusting that ultimate person. As we come closer to him in this trust walk, we are drawn by concentric circles closer to each other. Unity is a by-product of the faith journey. The reconciliation Paul speaks of is God's master plan for all things. As I respond and say yes and come closer to him, I look around me and discover my brother and sister, also members of God's household.

Having made that initial faith commitment, the next step is repentance. That's an old-fashioned word that seems unfamiliar and somewhat threatening these days, but it's simple enough. I once heard a story of how they used to catch monkeys. Narrow-necked bottles full of colored marbles were staked out in a clearing in the jungle. Monkeys, curious beings that they are, would soon appear and stick their hands into those bottles to grab a fistful of those interesting objects. They couldn't get their hands out without letting go of the marbles, which they were unwilling to do. And so the hunters would simply snatch them up and put them in cages. Repentance requires letting go of all the destructive and counterproductive things in our lives. Jesus tells us to let go of those things we're hanging onto so tightly and follow him. You have to take your hand out of the bottle if you are to be free to respond.

In Ephesians 3:11-13, Paul speaks of God's "eternal purpose which he accomplished in Christ Jesus our Lord. In him and through faith in him we may approach God with freedom and confidence. I ask you, therefore, not to be discouraged because of my sufferings for you, which are your glory." Having made the investment of faith then, and having let go of all those lesser loyalties and the things that keep us from being and doing all that we're meant to, we are to have boldness and confidence. If we believe in the lordship of Christ, anything is possible. We can dream big dreams for our lives, for our community, and for the world. We can witness with boldness to people who are not Christians. We can dare to risk losing a friend in order to speak a word for God. For if our faith investment is in our friends, we're on shaky ground indeed.

One of the many stories told about President Franklin Roosevelt concerns an incident that took place when he was governor of New York State. On the way to his office with a friend, he passed through the reception area where a fairly large group of people were waiting to see him. He paused long enough to tell a very old and not very funny joke. Later, in his private office, his friend inquired, "Mr. Roosevelt, why did you tell that group of people such an old joke?" "I wanted to see who laughed," said the president. "Everybody who laughed wants something from me." FDR was testing his colleagues. If you decide to tell a friend about Jesus, you may be testing the relationship. Paul promises us boldness and confidence.

Every Friday morning, I meet with a small group of men to read the Bible and share and pray. All six are employed in the secular world. One is a builder, one an engineer, one a lawyer, one a sales representative, one a coach, and one a manager. We're wrestling right now with what it means to belong to Jesus as we relate to other Christians in the marketplace. One of the men recently shared that he had been having a business problem with someone he knew to be a devout Roman Catholic. He did a bold thing. He went to his colleagues and said, "Listen, I know you're a devout Catholic. I'm a Presbyterian. Both of us are accountable to Jesus Christ. Why don't we pray about this problem we're having and see what he would say about it?" Even if every church in the land were crammed with believers every Sunday, our lives would not be significantly affected until we all started to relate to each other and work together under the lordship of Christ.

Paul promised confidence. We need never worry and wonder about our salvation. To mask our anxieties about eternity, we make these terrible jokes. I heard one about two men who lived in the same condominium complex, both with the same name—Paul Johnson. One was a sales representative and one a Presbyterian minister. The sales rep was sent on a business trip to Brazil, and he was kept so busy he didn't even have time to write home. He finally sent a cable, which was delivered not to his wife, but to the other Mrs. Johnson, whose preacher husband had died two days earlier. All the cable said was, "Arrived safely, heat unbearable." The jokes about heaven and hell are endless, but you and I never have to worry about our eternal future. If our salvation depended on our ethics, creeds, or politics, we would never make it. But our confidence is in Jesus Christ, who has redeemed us and purchased our reconciliation and our salvation.

In his letter Paul continued, "For this reason I kneel before the Father, from whom his whole family in heaven and on earth derives its name. I pray that out of his glorious riches he may strengthen you with power through his Spirit in your inner being, so that Christ may dwell in your hearts through faith. And I pray that you, being rooted and established in love, may have power, together with all the saints, to grasp how wide and long and high and deep is the love of Christ, and to know this love that surpasses knowledge—that you may be filled to the measure of all the fullness of God" (Eph. 3:14-19).

Paul promised that if our faith is in Jesus, we have riches. I charge you to spend those riches. Don't hoard them. Go out and write some checks on them. See whether or not his "glorious riches" are sufficient. You and I are strengthened with might through the Spirit. He dwells in our hearts. Where we go, he goes by his gracious choice. You and I are rooted in love. We can comprehend with all the saints the love of Christ which surpasses knowledge.

You can be filled with all the fullness of God. Quantitatively, there is no more of God in a huge congregation than there is in one believer, because God cannot be divided. When you are filled with the fullness of God, you have it all.

3

Terms of the Call

We might say that the first three chapters of Ephesians deal with doctrinal matters—*what* to believe. The next three chapters take up more practical concerns—*how* to live our lives. In other words, in this section we find the application of those doctrinal truths set forth earlier. The first verse of Chapter 4 is the cornerstone for all we've talked about so far and is the theme idea through all the succeeding chapters: "As a prisoner for the Lord, then, I urge you to live a life worthy of the calling you have received." Paul calls us to holy living. The word *holy* simply means "set apart." When you respond to God's call by committing yourself to the ultimate person, you are set apart to be someone in whom the Lord lives and through whom he ministers.

We are to lead a life worthy of the calling we have received: "Be completely humble and gentle; be patient, bearing with one another in love. Make every effort to keep the unity of the Spirit through the bond of peace. There is one body and one Spirit—just as you were called to one hope when you were called—one Lord, one faith, one baptism; one God and Father of all, who is over all and through all and in all" (Eph. 4:2-6).

Paul suggests here that there are three marks of holy living, of being set apart. They are love, peace, and unity. I would suggest that the first two are not all that difficult, especially if you choose a contemplative life. I often feel tempted to join some order where tranquility and regimen are emphasized and where one can live in harmony with other like-minded people. Ideally, there would be no difficult relationships. It would be just the Lord and I and a handful of folk who share my beliefs and goals. In a setting like that it might be easy to feel full of love and peace. But Paul added a third ingredient: being the body of Christ together in unity, to be in close relationship with other Christians of different nationalities, political systems, or ethical concerns. And that presents problems for us.

Holy living may seem like an impossible goal to most of us, but let's examine what it entails. What are these set apart, different people supposed to do and be? Paul goes on to tell us, "It was he who gave some to be apostles, some to be prophets, some to be evangelists, and some to be pastors and teachers, to prepare God's people for works of service, so that the body of Christ may be built up . . . " (4:11-12). It seems we have been set apart, called to holy living, in order to be ministers. One of the logos in our Seattle church is, "Every believer a minister" (1 Peter 2:19). If you're a Christian, you have no choice about it. You do have choices about where, how, when, and to whom you minister. God can and will direct and guide us about all of that.

Ministry is, in its essence, laying down your life for others. That does not necessarily mean martyrdom or being killed for a cause. It's living for a cause, living sacrificially, opening your heart and your pocketbook, being transparent and vulnerable, giving the affirmation and material assistance necessary to help our brothers and sisters become all they are meant to be.

At a staff lunch last year, we were asked to name a person, outside of an immediate family member, who was used by God to transform our lives at some point. Further, what exactly did that person do? The behaviors mentioned by the 30 or 40 people there were so ordinary. They turned out to be things that any of us are capable of—things like, "he/she took time with me . . . believed in me . . . listened to me." We may not be able to control our feelings or attitudes, but we can control our behavior, and that's what God can use to change somebody else's life.

An unusual research project was done at Duke University Medical School some years back. Over a one-year period, incoming patients were asked this question: "When you discovered you were ill, was there someone other than a medical person to whom you turned for help?" Oddly enough, the same 39 names kept cropping up. People from diverse backgrounds were seeking out this same fairly small group of lay people to find help for medical problems. The researchers called these unusual folks together to affirm their special ministry and to put them in touch with each other. They were in ministry, whether they were aware of it or not.

The holy living to which we are called centers in ministry, but it also requires purity. Paul spelled this out beginning with verse 17 of Chapter 4: " . . . you must no longer live as the Gentiles do. . . . Having lost all sensitivity, they have given themselves over to sensuality so as to indulge in every kind of impurity. . . . You were taught, with regard to your former way of life, to put off your old self, which is being corrupted by its deceitful desires; to be made new in the attitude of your minds; and to put on the new self, created to be like God in true righteousness and holiness." Paul is not saying that we can achieve perfection in this life. But we are to embrace the new nature that God has given us— a nature that is pure and holy, created in Christ's image. We are to receive this new nature as God's gift, to "put it on" like a brand-new set of clothes, and not give the old, sinful nature a chance to control us. *That* goal is attainable, while perfection is not.

Temptations are with us all the time, particularly in the area of impurity. A young priest is said to have gone to his father confessor, the senior priest in the parish, and said, "Father, at what age does a priest cease to be troubled by the sins of the flesh?" After some thought, the old priest answered, "I'll tell you, my son, I wouldn't trust myself until I was dead three days." We're not talking about a life where temptations no longer affect us. We're talking about a life in which we are striving to live out the new, pure nature and fighting against the old nature, with no rationalizations for our failures.

We're all familiar with the arguments for and against pornography. Can we control what other people see and read without interfering with their constitutional rights? It seems to me that for Christians, at least, pornography is especially deadly because it is opposed to the purity to which God calls us. It fills our minds with unsavory thoughts and desires.

Most of us are haunted by memories of shameful episodes from our past that we wish we could erase. Let's remember what happened when the Lord spoke to Isaiah. He was sitting in the sanctuary, just as most of us do Sunday after Sunday, when he saw the Lord seated on a throne: "Woe to me!" he cried. "I am ruined! For I am a man of unclean lips, and I live among a people of unclean lips, and my eyes have seen the King, the Lord Almighty." Then one of the angels took a coal from the altar and touched his lips, and he was made clean. So when the Lord said, "Whom shall I send? And who will go for us?" Isaiah could say, "Here am I. Send me!" (Isa. 6:1-8).

That is the expulsive power of a new affection. There are things that have been polluting our minds that we can't seem to escape—not just the memory of past sins, but the every-day pollution from novels, movies, or television. We come into God's presence, and the power of his love erases the chalkboard. Like Isaiah, we are touched with a burning coal and sent forth pure and clean again.

Beginning with the 25th verse of Chapter 4, Paul goes on to give us 12 commandments for holy living. Let's make a list of them. Many of us are list-makers. Tacked on our refrigerators or bulletin boards are three ways to improve our marriages, four ways to raise our children, and five steps to a better devotional life. Those of us who love lists need to get this one of Paul's firmly in our minds.

Holy living begins, first of all, with *speaking the truth to our neighbors*. We often waffle on that by presenting just one side of the truth. President Harry Truman, known as "Give 'Em Hell Harry," was once asked about that nickname. "I don't give 'em hell," he protested. "I just speak the truth, and it sounds like hell." Paul was adamant that saints set apart for holy living should speak only the truth. It seems to me that our society has fallen into some unfortunate doublespeak to obscure the truth. I read that the poor are now being called the "pre-rich." The most enormous arsenal in the world is referred to as "a peacekeeping force." When someone dies we euphemistically say that they have passed away, as if they had floated off on some mysterious cloud.

The second commandment is to *be angry*. "In your anger, do not sin" (v. 26). Wait a minute. Why does holy living include being angry? If you repress your anger, you will either pay an emotional price, or you will eventually express it inappropriately or to the wrong people. Feelings, even feelings of anger, are neither good nor bad, neither moral nor immoral. You can't control your feelings. But you *can* control your behavior. Don't stifle and deny and lie about your feelings of anger. At the same time, don't let the sun go down on your anger. Don't nurse it and plan vengeance. Rather, apologize, make restitution, and move on.

The third commandment is *don't steal*. I venture to say that no one who is trying to take his or her faith seriously would steal money openly. But there are many forms of theft. We are not to plagiarize what someone else has written, or take credit for what someone else has done. We are to pay fair wages if we're employers, and do a fair day's work as employees. We are not to exploit someone else's circumstances for our own gain.

There is a lot of talk these days about white-collar crime. That is just as off-limits for a Christian as any other kind of crime. I read about a contractor who called on a government official with a proposal. "In appreciation for the business you've given us, I'm planning to give you a sports car," said the contractor. The official was indignant. "I can't accept a sports car. That would violate my values, my principles, my ethical code." "I understand how you feel," the contractor said. "Why don't I sell it to you for $10." "In that case," the official responded, "I'll take two." We are all masters at finding ways to rationalize and excuse our behavior. Paul's word is simple. *Don't steal*.

The fourth commandment is to *clean up your speech*. Obviously this means no profanity. But the "unwholesome talk" Paul warns against has many guises, including ethnic jokes, put-down comments, and bragging. Gossip is particularly unwholesome because it can be the means of destroying someone else. It doesn't matter if the gossip is true or false. Dante reserved the lowest place in hell for gossips. Someone commented to a friend, "I didn't gossip about him. It must have been the people I told." It's hard to resist those conversations that begin with, "Have you heard? . . . ." Paul says we are to try. We need to clean up our speech.

The fifth commandment deals with *bitterness*. Sometimes it's hard not to be bitter. You may feel justified in bitterness if, for example, you are party to a divorce that you did not want. Of if you are single and feel you have not had the opportunities for marriage that others have had. And all of us who are married, no matter how happily, are bitter some of the time. There's enough reason for any of us to say, "I didn't get what I wanted or deserve." Paul is suggesting that nobody did, and bitterness will destroy us. Some people pursue happiness, others create it. We create happiness when we're able to put aside all bitterness and make the most of our circumstances, whatever they are.

The call to holy living includes *being kind*. That's number six. Sometimes I think kindness is the number one Christian virtue. How I wish I were kinder and had been kinder over the years to my wife, my children, my friends, my colleagues, my parents. I am not by nature a kind person. I'm critical, fault-finding, and judgmental. Paul says to me, "Larson, you are set apart for holy living. Be kind." When you are discussing someone else's faults, it's difficult not to put your thumb on the scales and make them even weightier.

Last fall, after several years of renting ski equipment, I went out to buy some skis and boots and bindings. The salesman asked first of all what kind of skier I was. I was hard-pressed to describe my degree of competence. "I'm a . . . a . . . ." "I know what you are," he said. "You're an aggressive intermediate." He had hit it exactly right. My wife laughs at me for going down the difficult trails, snow-plowing all the way and looking ridiculous. But I guess I'm an aggressive intermediate in Christian living as well. I'm not an expert. I want with all my heart to be God's person, but my lack of skill on some of the "slopes" Paul listed seriously hinders my progress.

The seventh commandment concerns *fornication and sexual immorality*. In other words, there is to be no sexual intercourse outside of marriage. Paul warned against all of the things that lead to sexual immorality, such as obscenity and coarse jokes. We Christians are a minority in the land today, just as the Christians of the first century were. We are to march to a different drummer. The fact that society accepts promiscuous behavior or casual sex is irrelevant.

Dr. Victor Klein, a psychologist at the University of Utah, has done research on how pornography affects us. He traces four clear stages of development. First, there is the initial addiction, then there's the escalation of that addiction. Next, desensitization takes place—sex is mechanical rather than relational. The final and fourth reaction to this constant stimuli is often a brutal act. That is why pornography is such a powerful tool of the powers of darkness. It leads to sexual immorality, fornication and, in extreme cases, sexual crime.

Number eight is a call to *live in the light*. Don't do in secret anything you wouldn't do in the open. Paul's letter urges us to expose the deeds of darkness. That's a large order as we think about the many places in our society where darkness threatens light—from poverty and crime on to global issues such as apartheid, political repression, or the threat of nuclear war.

Number nine—*make the most of your time*. This does not mean we are to be compulsive, driven workaholics. Perhaps we need to do less and do it better. Our lives should reflect a healthy rhythm, with time for recreation and work, worship and prayer. At a dinner party this past year I got into conversation with a parishioner I hadn't personally met before. He told me he operates a large management service with 200 employees reporting directly to him. I said, "What a stress-filled job that must be! How do you handle it?"

His wife had been following the conversation, and interrupted by saying, "I'll tell you how he does it. A few years ago at a conference he heard one of the speakers claim that spending five minutes a day reading the Bible would change your life. He made a promise to the Lord to do that and has never missed a single day since." It *has* changed his life. I think Jay has found the secret of using his time wisely. As he makes God the focus of his day, he gets perspective on the stress and pressure of his job.

Number ten is *don't get drunk*. There are Christians who would like to expand that into a simple, "Do not drink." You may remember that in Genesis Eve was guilty of wanting to expand on God's simple instructions not to eat of the fruit of one particular tree. In recounting the conversation to the serpent, she told him they were not even to *touch* the tree. I think she was guilty of wanting to believe God's demands were so harsh and exacting that no reasonable person could be expected to follow them. It's a rationale for disobedience that we're all guilty of sometimes. We can find no clear-cut call for temperance in these verses. Paul simply says, "Don't get drunk."

Number eleven is more positive: *be filled with the Spirit*. Paul tells us how. We are to read the Scriptures, praise, and sing. I grew up in a home where my zealous Christian mother was always singing hymns. Her voice wasn't particularly good, but it was loud. She filled the house with the Lord's praises. Sing hymns and praises, no matter what kind of a voice you have. Maybe you can't make the choir, but you can sing in the shower and a good many other places.

Paul's final commandment is to *give thanks always for everything*. It's taken me a lifetime to learn the wisdom of that. Peter DeVries has said, "We all learn by experience, but some of us have to go to summer school." I've had to go to summer school every year for many years to understand this simple truth. When you praise God *in* everything (not *for* everything) power is released. God dwells in the praises of his people.

Having gone through that list, holy living may seem to you difficult, to say the least. Let's remember again what Paul tells us in the opening paragraph of this magnificent letter. We are chosen, predestined, redeemed and forgiven, and the grace God has lavished on us makes all things possible.

4

A Call to Peace
and a Call to War

In his book *The One Minute Manager*, Kenneth Blanchard gives a simple, one-minute formula for being a better manager. He advises us to give frequent, one-minute shots of praise where it's deserved and one-minute shots of criticism where it's deserved. Workers, he claims, thrive on both.

It seems to me that in the last half of Ephesians, Paul gives us a course in one-minute sainthood. We've discussed the 12 specific commandments for holy living, but the letter concludes by highlighting two major themes that largely sum up our task as set-apart saints. We are to make peace with one another and we are to fight the powers of darkness. Too often we find ourselves fighting each other and making peace with the devil.

Our mandate for making peace is spelled out in Chapter 5, verse 21: "Submit to one another out of reverence for Christ." Then Paul discusses how to do that as husbands and wives, parents and children, slaves and masters. Husbands and wives are to be subject to one another, which is what love is all about at its best. To love is to serve, to be available, to sacrifice one's self.

Paul begins this section with a word to wives: ". . . submit to your husbands as to the Lord." A wife is to submit, not because her husband is superior or deserving or all-wise, but because that's what love does. Husbands are similarly commissioned in verse 25: ". . . love your wives, just as Christ loved the church and gave himself up for her. . . ." Christ submitted himself unto death for the sake of the church. He came to bless us, to give us life eternal, and we crucified him. He submitted himself and we despised him, forsook him, abused him, and denied him. That's a powerful role model for any Christian husband. It is only as each partner in a marriage submits to the other that a genuine love relationship is possible.

Someone told me that the Aztec Indian word for *wife* is an ideogram, a symbol or picture that illustrates the concept, "one who owns a man." There are wives who operate on that principle. Some of us live in terror of displeasing our spouse. A man congratulated a friend at a party on his seemingly happy marriage. "Yes, it really is," was the answer. "Don't you ever have any disagreements?" the first man asked. "Yes, of course we do, but we resolve them very quickly. I don't tell her about them."

That is not the kind of submission Paul is urging us to practice, to never object and never complain. There are bound to be disagreements. One psychologist said that the real test of whether a marriage is happy is whether or not the two of you can make a bed together. Does one have to tell the other what to do (pull the sheet tighter, make a hospital corner, lift this end, etc.)? He said the ideal is that two people are so in sync that each knows how the other wants the task done.

George Bernard Shaw, noted writer and cynic, said in the

beginning of his book *Getting Married*, "When two people are under the influence of the most violent, most insane, most delusive and most transient of passions, they are required to swear that they will remain in that excited, abnormal, and exhausting condition continuously until death do them part." Those intense, passionate feelings that you have at the beginning are not going to be constant. They are not supposed to be. But lasting love depends on wanting the other's best interest to such a degree that you are willing to give up your own interests, at least a significant part of the time.

Nathaniel Hawthorne, the great American writer, apparently had that kind of marriage. He came home in despair one day to tell his wife, Sophia, that he had been fired from his job at the customs house. Her response? "That's wonderful. Now you can start that great book that I've always believed you would write." He was scornful. "How can we live for a year while I do this writing?" With that, Sophia opened a drawer and took out a hoard of cash. Hawthorne demanded to know where she had gotten it. It seemed she had been saving a little bit of the household money every week for just such a time. She believed in his genius and was making plans to give him the freedom to write. In the next year, *The Scarlet Letter* was completed. All of us have times when we suffer defeats and disappointments. In the kind of marriage Paul is promoting, our spouses will say, "Let's see what God can do with this new opportunity."

Paul directed his attention next to parents and children. All of us have had parents or parental figures. Many of us are parents. Children are to obey their parents in the Lord. That does not refer to adult children, but to young children still living at home under their parents' care and protection. When children arrive at the age of consent, somewhere between 18 and 21, we parents need to let go of them just as the prodigal son's father did. Even if it means their ruination, we have no choice but to let go of them. The Fifth Commandment given to Moses is to honor your mother and father, and Paul reminds us of that here. We're to do that at any age. But for adult children, that does not necessarily mean obedience. When Jesus was a man of 30, his mother came to him and asked him to cease his ministry and come home with her. He refused because he had a higher allegiance to his heavenly Father. Nevertheless, he honored her. In those dying moments on the cross, his thoughts were for her and her welfare.

I've always been intrigued with verse 4 of Chapter 6, which says, "Fathers, do not exasperate your children. . . ." Mothers are not mentioned, and I'm not certain if that's because they are unlikely to exasperate their children or because they ought to be free to do so. At any rate, there's a fine line, it seems, between exasperating our children and correcting them. It's not easy.

Recently *The Wall Street Journal* carried a story about a fourth-grade class in Wilmette, Illinois. Most of the girls in this class of nine-year-olds were on diets, some even suffering from anorexia and bulimia. Apparently the boys in the class had made it clear they didn't like fat girls. How does a parent deal with that situation? How do you intervene when your child is caught in some ridiculous, destructive peer pressure that may become life-threatening? We're not to exasperate, but we have to find firm methods to correct.

Woodrow Wilson's parents must have been exasperated by him. He was 9 before he learned the alphabet and 11 before he was able to read. Wilson never had a job until he was 30, and in those years he lived at home with his parents. Don't you think his dad occasionally said, "Hey, son, when are you going to get out and make something of your life?" Wilson finally did get out of the house, first of all to be president of Princeton University and eventually to be president of our country. It's not easy to put up with an apparent loser without exasperating or being exasperated. One father said, "I want for my children all those things I never had—'As' on my report card." We lay goals on our children that we could not attain ourselves. When you are a parent of teenagers and going through all that violent turmoil with someone not quite an adult and not quite a child, you need a lot of help.

There's plenty of that available these days. By comparison, Paul's advice seems pretty sketchy. Even Miss Manners, that prim and proper authority on behavior, has a book on childrearing. She says, "Every child is born ignorant and oafish and is civilized by two things: example and nagging. It takes eighteen years of constant work to get one into presentable enough shape so that college will take him or her off your hands for the winter season. And it can easily take another ten years of coaching and reviewing before someone will consent to take the child on permanently."

We get further advice from the actor Ricardo Montalban, who wrote in a letter to his son: "In this house we do not have a democracy. I did not campaign to be your father. You did not vote for me. We are father and son by the grace of God, and I accept that privilege and awesome responsibility. In accepting it, I have an obligation to perform the role of a father. I am not your pal. Our ages are too different. We can share many things, but we are not pals. I am your father. This is one hundred times more than what a pal is." Obviously there is no definitive word yet on how to raise your children. Paul's suggestion is simple and all-encompassing, "Don't exasperate them." Instead, "bring them up in the training and instruction of the Lord" (v. 4).

Paul continues with advice to slaves and masters. "Slaves, obey your earthly masters with respect and fear. . . . And masters, treat your slaves in the same way. Do not threaten them, since you know that he who is both their Master and yours is in heaven . . . " (vv. 5, 9). It's still timely advice. There are no longer slaves in our society, but all of us are servants in the workplace and elsewhere. All of us have to answer to someone. Most of us are masters as well. We are in charge of children or employees or task groups of some kind. Even captains of industry must answer to a board of directors and to stockholders. In a good many matters they must answer to the government. Our president has masters—the American people and the Congress, to name just a couple. Even the most powerful man on earth is under authority. As a pastor, I have to answer to my congregation and to its elders. We're all in both the master and servant roles. Paul tells us to be kind to those under us and faithful to those over us. Love them. Make peace with them. Be good to them. As Christians we are all accountable to the one who is our Lord.

A recent government study indicates that the single most important factor in longevity is joy in the workplace. The people who are most happy in their work live the longest. They probably also make the most money and have the most time to spend it. I don't know a better way to have joy in the workplace than to follow Paul's advice: "Serve whole-heartedly, as if you were serving the Lord" (v. 7).

This remarkable letter ends with a clear call to take a stand against the devil's schemes. We are to "put on the full armor of God so that you can take your stand against the devil's schemes" (v. 11). That's who our real enemy is, not our spouse or our parents or our children, however difficult they may be. Our enemy is not our neighbor or employer or business competitor, however nasty or vindictive they may be. We are to make peace with all those people. Our battle is with the adversary, and against that adversary we need to wage a constant, holy war.

Let us not be deflected into doing battle with each other. In 1917, on the very day when the Bolshevik party was meeting in Russia to plan its strategy for the overthrow of the government, the leaders of the Russian church were gathered in the same city. They were arguing and they were angry and they were calling one another names. At issue was whether the candles in the sanctuary should be 18 inches long or 22 inches long. They were fighting the wrong battle, and so are we much of the time. We fall into opposing factions on a building committee or a stewardship committee and we forget that our warfare is with the adversary.

We can easily fall into one of two traps. We can focus too much on the devil, or we can deny the devil's existence. We're more likely to do the latter. As Dr. Karl Menninger said in his book, *Whatever Became of Sin?*, we are in a time when all antisocial, destructive behavior is attributed to mental or psychological aberrations. Yet there is something in the human psyche that cannot be accounted for so neatly. It is in you and in me, and when it operates collectively, as it did in Nazi Germany, seven million people can be killed in a Holocaust. That's corporate evil. That is not a mistake of judgment or the result of mass hysteria or a national superiority complex.

There are any number of similar examples. We cannot write them off as the isolated results of disturbed or deranged personalities. In Haiti the Duvaliers piled up their millions at the expense of the poorest nation in the world. Mr. Marcos robbed and raped the wealth of the Philippines while the populace lived in desperate poverty. How do we explain the situation in Ethiopia? The world pours in aid to help those who are starving while that nation's government hinders the effort because it is not politically expedient to keep those people—who are largely political foes—alive. We have to take seriously the fact that we are dealing with the principalities and powers of darkness. That prince of darkness is using every possible weapon in this warfare. Often he uses our very TV sets, with their constant excesses of violence and sex and destruction.

A pastor friend of mine is deeply involved in the fight against pornography, and he recently sent me something called "The Pornographer's Creed," a list of what pornographers would seem to believe: (1) that personal freedom and pleasure are the ultimate good; (2) that sexual pleasure and promiscuity are the way to a new life, fulfillment, and actualization and involve no long-term detrimental effects physically, mentally, or relationally; (3) sex is desirable with anyone at any time in any way that you wish; (4) promiscuity is assumed; marital fidelity and premarital self-discipline are mocked and belittled in countless magazines and films; (5) promiscuous sexual behavior is assumed to be more exciting and challenging than marital love; (6) freedom of speech as expressed in the First Amendment protects the right to copulate publicly and to describe or depict any sex act in print, on video tape, or over cable.

I'm sure pornographers would deny that this is their creed, but we must admit that people are selling all those ideas to the public in the slickest disguises, and in no way are those people serving the forces of light.

Paul closes Chapter 6 with a stirring description of the tools of war. He writes, "Therefore put on the full armor of God, so that when the day of evil comes, you may be able to stand your ground, and after you have done everything, to stand. Stand firm then, with the belt of truth buckled around your waist . . ." (vv. 13-14). It needs to be said that armor is *not* for defense. We don't put on our armor to hide in the basement. We put on armor to go out and engage the enemy. We are exhorted to wage a holy war against anything that dehumanizes and debases God's creatures who are made in his image.

The first piece of armor guards our most vulnerable place—our loins—and it is truth. It is the ultimate weapon against the father of lies, and a liar he is. He accuses us with his lies. He says we're dumb, no good, beyond help. The truth is that Jesus Christ died for us. We are of supreme worth. Wear that truth around your most vulnerable place.

The next piece is the breastplate, and it is righteousness. The second chapter of James's letter explains what that is. "'Abraham believed God, and it was credited to him as righteousness,' and he was called God's friend" (v. 23). Righteousness is believing God, believing that he is bigger than the sin in and around us. On our feet we are to wear the gospel of peace. Our shoes are the gospel of peace, and shoes are for walking. If there is someone you are not at peace with, put on those shoes and walk over and see him or her. Put on those shoes and call someone to say, "I'm sorry. Forgive me. I love you." Put the gospel of peace on your feet and walk your way into reconciliation.

An essential piece of the armor is the shield of faith. Your faith in Christ will deflect the darts of the enemy. Next, take salvation for a helmet. A helmet is to protect your head, and it was also, in Paul's time, a sign of victory. A conquering army always wore helmets. Wear that helmet. You are already redeemed. You are saved from the enemy who accuses you. God is on your side. Finally, take up the sword of the Spirit, the Word of God. It is a powerful weapon against all enemies.

It is an altogether awesome image, the whole armor of God. Certainly it was one more familiar to Paul's readers than it is to us. We have a harder time thinking in terms of armor and a holy battle as we go about our somewhat ordinary lives. But the battle is very real and God's resources are as well. Above all, we need not doubt the outcome. As Paul wrote in his letter to the Romans, "In all these things we are more than conquerors through him who loved us" (8:37).

5

Great
Expectations

In drawing a composite picture of holy living from the New Testament, we have another invaluable resource in a second letter by the apostle Paul—the epistle to the Philippians. If I were younger and smarter and could memorize one New Testament book, it would be that one. At the heart of that particular letter, it seems to me, is a wonderful word of hope. I believe God wants us to have a hope that can make a difference, a hope that can bring joy and thankfulness— in other words, great expectations.

Philippians is, in one sense, more a love poem than it is a logical treatise. Max Beerbaum, the great writer, once introduced a friend of his to another brilliant writer. Later the friend remarked to Beerbaum that he found it hard to believe that someone who seemed so scatterbrained could be such a gifted writer. Beerbaum replied, "Ah, but he has brains to scatter."

The apostle Paul was anything but scatterbrained, but in

this letter we find a scattering of brief thoughts, not as tightly organized as usual. He was not writing a Ph.D. thesis, complete with footnotes. Out of his great mind and heart and spirit, he poured forth his concerns to his favorite group of people, the saints at Philippi.

The opening verses are a testament to his love and affection for his readers. "I thank my God every time I remember you. In all my prayers for all of you, I always pray with joy because of your partnership in the gospel from the first day until now. . . . It is right for me to feel this way about all of you, since I have you in my heart; for whether I am in chains or defending and confirming the gospel, all of you share in God's grace with me. God can testify how I long for all of you with the affection of Christ Jesus. And this is my prayer: that your love may abound more and more in knowledge and depth of insight, so that you may be able to discern what is best and may be pure and blameless until the day of Christ . . ." (1:3-5, 7-10).

Paul began this letter to his beloved church by telling them what they should aim at and hope for. This same theme is underscored in the third chapter, where Paul writes, "Forgetting what is behind and straining toward what is ahead, I press on toward the goal to win the prize for which God has called me heavenward in Christ Jesus" (vv. 13-14). That's where Paul's hope was centered, and that's the hope to which he challenged his brothers and sisters in Philippi.

If you were to tell me what your hopes are for your life, I think I could predict just about how happy you are going to be. So often life breaks down because of our false expectations. Certainly a good many marriages do. We call it the "Cinderella Syndrome." Life may be difficult and unrewarding, but we think that marriage will change all that. We'll live happily ever after. Marriage to the right person is a great gift, but it doesn't solve our problems. When they occur, we tend to blame our spouse, saying, "You are what's wrong with me. If you were different, I'd be happier."

I happen to live in one of the states where people are now caught up in the frenzy to win a sweepstakes or lottery. We think that large sums of money are the route to a trouble-free life. It's sobering to read the stories of some of the people who have won those prizes. They are unhappy and disillusioned. For some, winning the prize marked the beginning of drug or alcohol problems or the breakdown of lifelong relationships.

There are worthier goals, of course. We may want most of all to serve other people in some helping profession. That's good, but not good enough. We are being made increasingly aware of the occupational hazards of those professions—the drug-addicted physician, the burned-out pastor, the unscrupulous therapist.

I heard about an airplane passenger who turned to his seatmate just after takeoff and said, "Do you see that lake down there? When I was a small boy I used to sit in a flat-bottomed boat fishing, watching the planes take off and wishing I was flying in one of them. Now I fly out of here at least once a week and I look down and wish I was in that flat-bottomed boat fishing." When this man's hopes were realized, he found that wasn't what he was hoping for after all.

In their book, *Person to Person* (Pocket Books, 1971), Carl Rogers and Barry Stevens made these insightful comments about the human condition:

The most important thing is to have a career. The most important thing is to get married. . . . The most important thing is sex. The most important thing is to have money in the bank. The most important thing is to have everyone like you. The most important thing is to dress well. The most important thing is to be sophisticated and say what you don't mean and don't let anyone know what you feel. The most important thing is to be ahead of everyone else. The most important thing is a black seal coat and china and silver. The most important thing is to be clean. The most important thing is to always pay your debts. The most important thing is not to be taken in by anyone else. The most important thing is to love your parents. The most important thing is to work. The most important thing is to be independent. The most important thing is to speak correct English. The most important thing is to be dutiful to your husband. The most important thing is to see that your children behave well. The most important thing is to go to the right plays and read the right books. The most important thing is to do what others say. And others say these things.

When we read all of these goals one after the other, we see how unimportant most of these important things really are.

Certainly the most important thing is our relationship with God and our response to his call to holy living. But we can have false expectations about that as well. We tend to think that when we are born again, are Spirit-filled, and walk with the Lord, we will no longer have problems. We will no longer have doubts. We will no longer be old or poor or lonely. We will no longer be sinners. We will be loved. At the very least, we will always have a date on Saturday night. Unfortunately, none of those things are guaranteed in the life of faith. That's why Philippians speaks to us so poignantly.

This is Paul's most intimate and personal letter. He used the word *joy* more often in Philippians than in all of his other writings combined. He wrote as if he were a man who had it all writing to a church that had it all, but the facts would seem to give the lie to that. At the time he wrote this letter, about A.D. 61–63, Paul was in prison in Rome. He was alone and living on the gifts of friends. How could he have had it all? He wrote to a church that was largely lacking in material things. This church had been founded about 10 years earlier on Paul's second missionary journey, and I think the New Testament account of how that happened is relevant for any new church development program today. Let's review the events.

First of all, Paul went to Philippi at the direct guidance and intervention of the Spirit. He was prevented from going to Bithynia, and instead, in a vision, a man from Macedonia stood before him begging, "Come over to Macedonia and help us" (Acts 16:6-10). For the first time, the gospel went west into Europe. Paul was sent there as a result of a specific and timely vision.

As soon as he arrived, he went, as was his custom, to the place where the Jews worshiped. In this case, they were meeting on a riverbank (a common place of prayer for Jews in a city without a synagogue). He joined them and began to preach about Jesus, and the first person to hear and respond—the first European convert—was a woman.

She was not a typical woman of the time. Most were scarcely more than slaves or chattel. Lydia was a wealthy businesswoman. She sold and bought purple dye. Her openness to the gospel was extraordinary. On the first hearing, she decided she believed in this Messiah Paul proclaimed. She and all of her family were baptized. On the heels of that dramatic event, she invited Paul and his friends to come and stay in her house, and they did.

Today there are no ruins of a church at Philippi, nor, as far as we know, have there ever been. This most exciting of all the apostolic churches met in a home long since destroyed. I'm told there is a chapel along the riverbank, built to mark the place where the gospel first came to Europe, and where Lydia was baptized.

From this church in Lydia's house, Paul continued his preaching ministry. It was given impetus as the result of an unusual healing. A demented slave girl had taken to following Paul around, crying out without ceasing each time he spoke, "These men are servants of the Most High God, who are telling you the way to be saved" (Acts 16:17). After three days of this, Paul had had enough. In annoyance he turned and said to the spirit who was troubling her, "In the name of Jesus Christ I command you to come out of her!" And the spirit left her. It's comforting to know that Jesus' power was just as available to Paul when his motives were less than the best. Our prayers and our word of faith can change somebody's life whether we feel compassionate or not.

This young woman was liberated from her illness, and her owners, who had been making money as a result of her fortune-telling, were angry. They had Paul and Silas beaten and thrown into prison. Undaunted, even with their feet in stocks, the two of them were singing hymns of praise at midnight. Their exuberance amidst those dismal circumstances is unexplainable apart from God and his presence. In the middle of their singing an earthquake occurred.

We could call that an amazing coincidence. All the cell doors were opened. The jailer rushed to the scene in a panic, certain that all the prisoners had escaped. Under Roman law, he would have been executed for allowing them to escape, and he had his sword drawn, about to kill himself. Paul reassured him: "Don't harm yourself! We are all here." The jailer was so amazed by what he saw that he asked that famous question, as pertinent today as it was then, "What must I do to be saved?" Paul spoke the Word of God to him and to all his household, and they were all baptized that very night (Acts 16:25-33).

That's an interesting formula for new church development, isn't it? The first requirement is a vision. The next step is a wealthy convert in the church. Move from that to a miraculous healing done in public and, finally, on to the conversion of a nonreligious, establishment-type like the Philippian jailer. That's how this most exciting of all the apostolic churches began, and it is an intriguing progression of events. The first converts were a Jew (Lydia), a Roman (the jailer), and a Greek (the slave girl). The first church in Europe was made up of all three groups, people who had just one thing in common—Jesus Christ.

Dr. Wilfred Grenfell, famous pioneer missionary, was converted in London at the turn of the century, and he went on to start the first medical work in Labrador. He spent 40 years there among the Eskimos, other Indians, and a smattering of settlers. Occasionally he made speaking trips to acquaint people with the work in Labrador. On one such occasion, at a Congregational church in New England, he told about a Roman Catholic patient of his who had no prosthesis to replace her amputated leg. After the service, a woman said to him, "I'm Methodist, but my Presbyterian husband who died some years ago had an artificial leg. You can have it."

A good-fitting prosthesis is not easy to find, but, miraculously enough, when the woman in Labrador was fitted with this new leg, she could walk perfectly. Grenfell summed it up in this way: "When I, an Episcopalian, took that Presbyterian leg given to me by a Methodist woman in a Congregational church and fitted it on my Roman Catholic friend, it enabled her to walk perfectly." That's the ecumenical church at work. Some of the first seeds of that ecumenical church were planted in Philippi. A Jewish businesswoman, a Greek slave girl, and a Roman official became brothers and sisters in the household of faith.

We know that Paul made two subsequent visits to Philippi, and he summed up his hopes for them in the first chapter of his letter. His hope was that Christ would be proclaimed and that " . . . Christ will be exalted in my body, whether by life or by death. For to me, to live is Christ and to die is gain" (1:20-21).

Paul did not aspire to be a famous evangelist, friend and confidant of presidents and kings, though there is nothing intrinsically wrong with that. He didn't aspire to be a pope, a statesman and administrator for the church worldwide. He didn't aspire to preach in great cathedrals, to write for millions of readers, or even to be a guru to a devoted group of followers. Paul's hope was to be a part of the faithful family of Christ and to honor Christ by his living or by his dying.

Certainly Paul knew he would suffer. He had already done a good deal of that. As he wrote in verses 29-30, "For it has been granted to you on behalf of Christ not only to believe on him, but also to suffer for him, since you are going through the same struggle you saw I had, and now hear that I still have." As Christians we will suffer. We may be sick, poor, lonely, or old someday. We will certainly die. But our aim is to be a part of the body of Christ, blessing each other and being a blessing to the world.

A woman was complaining to her pastor about all of the hard things in her life. He tried to comfort her with those verses from the 10th chapter of first Corinthians: "No temptation has seized you except what is common to man. And God is faithful; he will not let you be tempted beyond what you can bear" (v. 13). Her response was, "Well, I wish God didn't have such a high opinion of me." I'm convinced the Lord has a high opinion of you and me. He knows how much we can bear. If our goal is a trouble-free life, without enemies and problems, we are headed for disappointment.

But if our hope is in that living body that will never die, that moves through the ages with surety and power, those hopes will be realized.

I've mentioned several times in sermons over the past years that it takes 10 "atta-boys" to equal one "you jerk." One parishioner responded to that remark with a letter. In intent, at least, it is not unlike this letter of Paul's to the church at Philippi. It begins, "Dear Bruce: Atta-boy, Atta-boy, Atta-boy," and continues through 20 "atta-boys." In other words, I have enough "atta-boys" on tap to cancel out two "you jerks." We might say this is the vein of Paul's letter to his friends at Philippi. He is saying, "Atta-boy. You can do it. Don't fail. Keep on keeping on." He knew God had great expectations for them, just as he does for you and me.

6

The Touch
of Love

A small town in Minnesota recently sponsored a contest, the object of which was to draw a *lutefisk* (*lutefisk* is a Norwegian word for a certain codfish recipe). The first prize went to a contestant who had drawn a pizza. I understand the problem, being Scandinavian. I would be hard pressed to describe a lutefisk, let alone draw one.

There are some other things in life that would be even more difficult to draw—love, for instance. More specifically, God's love for us and our love for one another. We would all draw something different, of course. But there are some particular pictures, familiar to us all, that perhaps begin to explain or describe love. There is that Boys' Town poster, used for years, of a ten-year-old arriving at Father Flanagan's famous home, carrying his six-year-old brother on his back, with the caption, "He ain't heavy. He's my brother." Another familiar picture hangs in many doctors' waiting rooms. It's the country doctor sitting up with a sick child who is lying in a makeshift bed of two chairs pulled together. It's obviously late and the anxious family is gathered around. That doctor is not merely making a house call. He's keeping a vigil in the hope that the child may take a turn for the better. It's a picture that grabs us, especially in today's impersonal world.

Your picture of love might be of a parent or family member—in many cases, a mother—who went way beyond the call of duty to love and provide for you. Mrs. John Wesley, mother of the founder of the Methodist church, had 11 children, and she was once asked which was her favorite child. She answered, "I love the one who's sick until he's well and the one who's away until he comes home."

Then there's Albrecht Dürer's famous black-and-white picture of the praying hands. That's one that still has the ability to move most of us. There's a remarkable story behind that painting. It seems that Albrecht and another young artist found themselves in financial difficulty and couldn't afford to stay in art school. It was decided that one of them would get some menial job to support the other. When one partner became a success, then the other would be able to study. Since Albrecht seemed the more talented of the two, his friend spent the next years doing all sorts of menial work. In the meantime, Albrecht completed his studies, began to sell his art, and was finally in a position to help his roommate. By that time, however, the hands of that self-sacrificing man were so gnarled and broken, he could no longer hold a brush. One fateful day, Albrecht came home to find his friend in prayer, and he started to sketch those now well-known hands, the hands that had made it possible for him to pursue his career. That's the picture that speaks so eloquently of love and faithfulness.

In the second chapter of Philippians, Paul draws love for us with a word picture. "Your attitude should be the same as that of Christ Jesus: who, being in very nature God, did not consider equality with God something to be grasped, but made himself nothing, taking the very nature of a servant, being made in human likeness. And being found in appearance as a man, he humbled himself and became obedient to death—even death on a cross!" (vv. 5-8). The incarnation is the most powerful portrayal of God's love for us. "For God so loved the world that he gave his one and only son . . ." (John 3:16). It is a love beyond our understanding.

Doesn't it seem preposterous that God would trust his one and only Son to human parents? A teenage mother had to change his diapers and nurse him. That is the wonder of the Christmas story. Sometimes, as I watch my son playing with his own baby son, I think about Joseph. Did he occasionally change a diaper and nuzzle that bare little belly and go "b-r-r-r-r"? Do you think Joseph ever lifted the baby Jesus high in the air over and over, while the infant giggled and squealed in delight? God's Son being tossed in the air by a doting and playful father—that's the astonishing implication of the Christmas message. God's Son was totally at the mercy of the world and its people, be they loving parents or hostile rulers.

One of our parishioners recently gave me a poem by a man named John Tabb, who died in 1909. Above the poem, there is a picture of a little boy, not unlike my own little grandson. He's crawling backward down a staircase. He's curly-headed and has the usual big, diaper-wrapped fanny. At the bottom of the stairs is a ball, and he is obviously going down to retrieve it. Here's the poem:

A little boy of heavenly birth, but far from home today,
Came down to find his ball, the earth,
    that sin has cast away.

Oh, brothers, let us one and all
Join in to give him back his ball.

Paul's message here is mind-blowing. He is not suggesting God chose a nice, little, Jewish baby and decided to make him the Messiah. This ball, the earth, belongs to him. And the Creator and ultimate Redeemer left heaven, came to earth, and was dependent on an earthly mother and father to meet his needs and to feed and care for him. Unless Mary and Joseph nurtured this baby lovingly and carefully, the baby would die. In the incarnation, God took on the flesh of his own creation.

I'm an unashamed creationist, and I happen to believe that God made the world in some mysterious way in six celestial days, however long those were. But even if you are an evolutionist, that theory doesn't explain the human race. At some point, something happened to our species that made us different from the other animals. Michelangelo gave us his version of that miraculous moment in that glorious paint-ing on the ceiling of the Sistine Chapel in Rome. We see the first being—in this case, Adam—reaching upward while God's finger stretches down. These two fingers touch, and the human race is born. God has breathed his Spirit into us and, unlike any other animal, we have the capacity for good and evil, for love and hatred.

God touched Mary. She didn't receive some inspirational message at the well in Nazareth. God interrupted the men-strual cycle of a young Jewish girl, and the proof was that weeks and months later she began to feel life inside her. Much of Jesus' ministry involved touch. The incarnate God, in full humanity in Jesus, touched a blind man, and he began to see—at first, imperfectly. He saw people as trees walking. Then Jesus touched him a second time. Perhaps you've experienced that kind of second touch in your life. Even though you were a Christian, perhaps you didn't see clearly who you were or who you were meant to be. You weren't able to see your neighbors and their needs. You may have had a second touch, and you may need a third or even a fourth. Throughout life, God continues to touch us.

Senator Charles Sumner, leader of the Abolitionist Movement during the Civil War, was once asked for a favor by Julia Ward Howe, the great composer. Would he help a friend of hers who was in trouble? "My dear Julia," said Sumner, "I am so busy with the Abolitionist Movement that I don't have time to take care of individual people." She said, "How remarkable, Charles! Even God hasn't reached that stage yet." God is still on your agenda and mine, touching us where we live and where we hurt.

There are some moving stories in the Gospels about the people who touched Jesus. One concerns the woman with an issue of blood, whom doctors had been unable to help. She was convinced that if she could just touch his garment, she would be healed—and she was. She was hoping for anonymity, but even with the crowds pressing around him, Jesus knew someone had touched him. He still does.

In the middle of a public dinner party, Mary Magdalene touched him. Forgiven and healed, she sought out Jesus while he was dining at the home of Simon, a Pharisee. With a year's worth of wages, she had purchased precious ointment with which she bathed his feet, wiping them with her hair. The host was offended, certain that Jesus was unaware that these ministrations were being performed by a person of ill repute. But Jesus assured Simon that he knew exactly who she was, and throughout all the history of the world, what she had done would be remembered.

In Philippians 2:4, Paul spells out some of the implications for those of us who believe that God in Jesus has touched us. "Each of you should look not only to your own interests, but also to the interests of others." We have a mandate to touch others in Christ's name, to take responsibility for those around us, and to serve their interests as well as our own. That can take many forms, of course—the most obvious being to care for those who are needy, sick, imprisoned, or oppressed. It's hard to do all that from some aloof and impersonal position. Sometimes our ministry includes physical touch—the laying on of hands.

People in the medical profession are becoming more and more aware that beyond medical and surgical skills, there is something therapeutic about the laying on of hands. One of our elders was in the hospital about a year ago with a serious heart condition. While waiting to see him, another man joined me in the waiting room. We discovered we were both calling on the same patient. This middle-aged man was wearing a badge that said, "Hug Therapist." I wanted to know what in the dickens a Hug Therapist was. It seems he had been hospitalized himself previously and found himself strangely helped by the people who stopped in and touched him or hugged him. "I could feel power coming into me," he said. "Now in my spare time, I visit friends and colleagues who are ill and do hug therapy." I decided then and there that there were going to be two such specialists calling on patients.

Some scientist in California has been trying to measure the power transmitted by a hug. She discovered that you need 4 hugs a day for survival, 8 for maintenance, and 12 to grow. It would behoove all of us to be hug therapists, in the business of giving and receiving 12 hugs a day.

Peter DeVries, one of my favorite authors, says, "Our business in life is not to see through one another; it's to see one another through." The laying on of hands is just one more way to see someone through—someone who is hurting, lonely, or in physical or mental pain.

Last year the newspapers carried a story about a man named Shorty Crandall. He had been living in the same mobile home park in Indiana for about 15 years. A man of 72, he received a Social Security check each month in the amount of $352. Obviously, he didn't have a lot of extra money. Yet two or three nights a week he'd go into the State Street Grill and buy a beer or two and just sit. According to the bartender, "He doesn't bother anybody. He's just a nice, old guy who sits there and drinks a beer." Well, one day Shorty surprised everyone by walking into his bank with no weapon and no disguise and announcing to his usual teller, "This is a robbery. Give me a bunch of money." The startled teller grabbed a fistfull of $10-dollar bills and handed them over. "Thank you," said Shorty. "I'll be at the State Street Grill if you need me." Of course, he was promptly arrested. He was found guilty and sent to jail, where, he claims, "It's not all bad." He's surrounded by people and has lots of friends. It's a bizarre story. Few of us would rob a bank simply to avoid being alone. But a good many people in this impersonal world of ours are literally dying of loneliness. Anything is better than the life they live. As we reach out and touch someone like that, include them in our lives, and become a part of theirs, we have the power to bring about positive change and to affect what happens to them. One dimension of holy living is touching people where they hurt.

Sometimes the touch of love is more verbal than physical. Sherman Rogers has written a book about logging in the Pacific Northwest. As a young man he worked in a logging camp, and on one occasion the boss needed to be away for a while and put Sherman in charge. "What exactly does that mean?" Sherman wanted to know. "Can I fire people?" "Yes," said the foreman, "And I know what you're getting at. You're going to fire Tony the first chance you get. I know he doesn't get along with anybody. He's nasty and he grumbles. But let me tell you something about Tony. He's been with me eight years. He's the first person to arrive on the job and the last to leave. Nobody has ever had an accident around Tony. His hill is always the safest one to work on."

On the first day of his new responsibilities, Sherman arrived at Tony's hill and announced he had been put in charge. "I suppose that means you're going to fire me," said Tony. "Actually, I was," said Sherman, "but the boss told me you're the best workman we have. He said you're the first to come and the last to leave, and there's never been an accident around you." Sherman was startled to see tears begin to flow down Tony's cheeks. "Why didn't he tell me that eight years ago?" he cried. Twelve years later Tony was the head of one of the largest logging companies in the area and he never failed to remind Sherman that it all began on the day he was told what the boss had said about him. We are all surrounded by people who have no sense of their importance or worth. Our touch, verbal or actual, may change a life.

Karl Menninger, the psychiatrist, was asked what someone should do who feels on the verge of a nervous breakdown. His advice? "Lock your house, go across the railroad tracks, find someone in need and do something for him." The call to holy living begins when God touches us. In his name, we are to reach out and touch our brothers and sisters. In Paul's words, "Each of you should look not only to your own interests, but also to the interests of others."

7

At the Heart
of Holy Living

A while back a product that had been around for almost a hundred years and billed itself as "the real thing" changed its formula. That seemed weird; after all those successful years, we were being told that the manufacturers had come up with something more real than the real thing. One of our neighbors in Seattle became famous as the consumer advocate for all of those people from all corners of our land who lamented the loss of the original real thing. Hooked on the real thing, they refused to accept the new thing. In a strange turn of events, this Seattle champion of the real thing was given three different blindfolded tasting tests by the press, and, it seems, he could not tell the real thing from the new thing. We are left wondering if the real thing is the new thing or the old thing.

The last chapter talked about pursuing the real thing in life. We all have a certain measure of valuable commodities, the first being our time, and then, in varying amounts, our energies, money, and creativity, and we exchange those in order to obtain something else. In a few cases, that "something else is fame and fortune," but for most of us, it is something more mundane, such as three meals a day and a roof over our head. Yet the world presents us with a smorgasbord of pursuits and pleasures, all claiming to be the real thing.

The choices are just as myriad in the religious world. There are those preachers (fortunately, a small number) who promise their followers affluence. They insist that God wants you to be a millionaire. If you worship their way, they'll tell you how to do it.

Then there are the gurus who give you permission to enjoy, to do whatever feels good, such as the Rajneesh. For others, the real thing in the religious world is marked by doctrinal certainty and theological exactitude. There is no shortage of fundamentalist churches who will interpret the Scriptures for you and tell you exactly what to believe and how to behave. If the whole idea of sin is anathema to you, Christian Science offers another route. For them, there is no sin and no illness. It's all in the mind.

There are those who think the real thing, religiously speaking, requires infallible guidance every day. Many of my friends in the Moral Rearmament movement believe that if you listen, God will speak to you clearly on a daily basis and you will know how to proceed without any wrong turns or errors of judgment. Perhaps you're seeking simplicity above all else. You could join a convent or monastery or one of the contemporary Protestant versions of that life-style. Then there are the eastern religions and their offers of enlightenment.

What, then, is the bottom line for those Christians of a biblical persuasion who are called to holy living and are trying to be New Testament saints with an authentic life-style? We are not offered perfect faith. None of the biblical men and women of either the Old or the New Testament had a perfect faith. We cannot claim to have perfect faith or even to be good. In the Scriptures, Abraham is praised for his exemplary faith. Abraham and Sarah left everything and followed God to a new land. And yet Abraham doubted and lied, and both he and Sarah laughed at God.

Romantically, we think that if we had only been present with Jesus in the flesh, our faith would be perfect. Peter and James and John traveled with him for three years. They were at the Mountain of Transfiguration when God revealed that their friend and teacher was, in fact, the Messiah. In spite of all that, Peter eventually denied his Lord, and James and John were given to squabbling over which one would have first place in the kingdom.

We like to think that perfect faith was possible beginning with the events at Pentecost. At Pentecost, the Holy Spirit came in power on all of the believers for the first time. Wind blew and fire appeared. They spoke in foreign tongues. Just days before that experience, the Lord had commanded them to go into all the world and make disciples of all nations. They didn't go. They stayed in Jerusalem until a persecution arose and they had to flee for their lives. Only then did they obey the Lord's command. Perfect faith, we find, is not the "real thing" for Christians then or now.

Even after we have given the Lord our lives, we still have days when it doesn't make sense. One of the psychiatrists in our congregation claims that some people are born with good "faith genes." It's easier for them to believe. Others of us are more like "doubting Thomas." But even if you are full of faith genes, there are days when you say, "Is it really true? Is it all worthwhile?"

In the Philippian letter, Paul poured out his heart to this

very special church, and he wrote about the real thing. "I consider everything a loss compared to the surpassing greatness of knowing Christ Jesus my Lord . . ." (3:8). According to Paul, only Jesus is the real thing.

I am pastor of a church in which some members are very conservative theologically, some, in fact, are fundamentalists. There are a good many theological liberals and a lot more somewhere in between the two. I don't see that as a problem. Our faith does not rest in liberal or conservative theology. Our faith rests in a person, the person of Jesus Christ. Faith is having a relationship with that person. That can encompass a fairly broad spectrum of theology, as long as the theology is centered on the person of Jesus Christ.

This relationship is a progressive one, and Paul outlined its three stages for the Philippian church and for us: "I want to know Christ and the power of his resurrection and the fellowship of sharing in his sufferings" (3:10). Think of these as three concentric circles. We are Christians first of all, not because we are better than other people or know more or are doctrinally sound. We are Christians because we *know* the person of *Jesus*. That is not left-brain, scientific knowledge. It is a right-brain, intuitive knowing, the kind that operates when we fall in love and marry. The outer circle, then, includes all those who know truth as a person.

That's a starting point. It's the point at which we receive new members into the church. Our hope is that those people who have said yes to Jesus and want to be our sisters and brothers in the faith will grow in that relationship. Paul says the next step is to know "the power of his resurrection." We may know him and yet be afraid to tap into his power and exercise it. We believers are a royal priesthood, and we are given power to listen and to love, to pray and to witness. We can expect miracles because we belong to someone whose limitless power is ours.

Finally, the smaller group inside those two concentric circles is made up of those who share in the fellowship of Jesus' suffering. We do that when we walk our faith into a hurting world. As we move out to listen and care and serve, we move into that inner circle Paul describes, and that is the apex of the real thing. Dietrich Bonhoeffer once said that "to be a Christian is to suffer with God in a godless world." That's how we enter into that fellowship of suffering that Paul wrote about.

The original charter for Harvard College, now Harvard University, contained these surprising words. "Let every student be plainly instructed and earnestly pressed to consider well that the main end of his life and studies is to know God and Jesus Christ . . . , and therefore to lay Christ in the bottom, as the only foundation of all sound knowledge and learning." Would that that same uncompromising Christian challenge was being extended to today's Harvard student!

My wife Hazel and I were in Hawaii last year with two dear, old friends, Norman and Ruth Peale. In our years in New York, working for an interdenominational, para-church ministry, we got to know these two extraordinary people. For 12 years now they have been holding a Thanksgiving conference in different parts of the world. Norman was the Sunday morning preacher for the 1100 attendees. Last year the ballroom was packed, and I was struck by the fact that this 87-year-old saint seemed undiminished in his powers. He spoke with vigor and volume. His enthusiasm and storytelling ability were unchanged. Few people have affected the world for Jesus as much as this one man. His books and his radio and TV broadcasts have introduced millions to Jesus, among them my own stepfather.

I'm always curious about people God has used so powerfully, and in Hawaii I had a chance to learn more about

Norman's beginnings. He told us all the following story. "My dad was a Methodist minister. When Haley's Comet came over the last time, I remember I was standing in the backyard with my brother and my dad, who always had a keen interest in science. That comet went right over our house in Cincinnati. I remember saying, 'Dad, do you think I'll still be around when Haley's Comet comes back?' I'll never forget his answer. 'Son, that isn't important. What's important is what you do with your life in the meantime.'"

He continued, "Every night my mother and dad came up to have prayers with my brother and me before we went to sleep. Women didn't pray aloud in those days, so dad did all the praying. Then mom would kiss and hug us and dad would tousle our hair and punch us in the chest and give us this parting shot: 'Remember, boys, stick with Jesus.'" That's the secret of Norman Peale's ministry and it's the secret of yours and mine. Just stick with Jesus.

At 14, my mother left her home in Sweden, said good-bye to her father and stepmother and 11 half-sisters and brothers, and went off to America. Her parting gift from her father, whose heart must have been breaking (for he would never see her again), was a Bible in which he had written two verses. The first is from the epistle of 3 John: "I have no greater joy than to know that my children walk in the truth." The second is a statement by Jesus from John's Gospel: "I am the way, the truth and the life." She put those same verses in my Bible as I went off to combat in World War II at age 17. Last Christmas I gave each of my own three children a Bible in which those two verses are inscribed. Our faith centers in Jesus. In a world of ever-changing loves and loyalties, claims and causes, he is the real thing.

One of my favorite poems is this familiar one by John

Oxenham. He sums up in beautiful prose the essence of what Paul wrote to the Philippians.

CREDO

Not what, but whom I do believe,
That, in my darkest hour of need,
Hath comfort that no mortal creed
To mortal man may give;—
Not what, but whom!
For Christ is more than all the creeds,
And his full life of gentle deeds
Shall all the creeds outlive.
Not what I do believe, but whom!
Who walkes beside me in the gloom?
Who shares the burden wearisome?
Who all the dim way doth illume,
And bids me look beyond the tomb
The larger life to live?—
Not what I do believe,
But whom!
Not what,
But whom!

8

A Call
to Rejoice

A full-page ad in *The Wall Street Journal* caught my attention last year. It was placed by United Technologies of Hartford, Connecticut: "Have you noticed the great difference between the people you meet? Some are as sunshiny as a handful of forget-me-nots. Others come on like frozen mackerel. A cheery, comforting nurse can help make a hospital stay bearable. An upbeat secretary makes visitors glad they came to see you. Every corner of the world has its clouds, gripes, complainers, and pains in the neck—because many people have yet to learn that honey works better than vinegar. You're in control of *your* small corner of the world. Brighten it. . . . You *can*." That's quite a message from a secular organization, placed in a secular journal and addressed to a secular audience.

In Philippians the apostle Paul gave his friends a similar message, except in much more biblical terms. "Rejoice in the Lord always. I will say it again: Rejoice!" We are to rejoice because God cares. We are loved and forgiven.

Even the secular world knows the importance of joy and the adverse effects of its absence. Christians ought to be even more aware of that. Joy is the authenticating mark of the true believer and the true church. I tell friends who are church-shopping in a strange city to look for that mark. In true worship, you ought to sense joy, even before you hear a note from the choir or a word from the pulpit. The aroma of gladness will tell you that God dwells and does business in that place. Teilhard de Chardin once said, "Joy is the surest sign of the presence of God." Personally, I find I distrust the dour saint.

Joseph Haydn was one of God's great gifts to the human race, a composer who captured so much of the mystery and wonder of God in his music. He was once asked why his music was so cheerful. "I cannot make it otherwise," he said. "I write according to the thoughts I feel. When I think upon God, my heart is so full of joy that the notes dance and leap, as it were, from my pen. And since God has given me a cheerful heart, it will be pardoned me that I serve him with a cheerful spirit." Haydn's awareness of God resulted in his being overwhelmed with joy.

More than 20 times in this short letter to the Philippians, Paul wrote rejoice, give thanks, give thanks, rejoice. We are to rejoice when we pray. Of course. We are talking to God, our Father and Creator. That is cause to rejoice. We are to rejoice in the gospel. The gospel is good news about a personal God who is omniscient and omnipresent and omnipotent and yet by whom we are loved and forgiven. How can we help but share that good news?

In his second chapter, Paul told the Philippians that they would make his joy complete by being one in spirit and purpose. We can rejoice that we belong to the household of God, to the family of believers, one body whose head is Christ. Paul told his readers to rejoice even if his life had to be poured out as a sacrifice. He told them that God was using even his imprisonment to advance the cause of the gospel. "It has become clear throughout the whole palace guard and to everyone else that I am in chains for Christ" (1:12). We can rejoice even when we feel we are being sacrificed for a cause.

Sometimes I try a little experiment as I walk down a busy city street. I try to look into the eyes and faces of the people coming toward me. It's enlightening, to say the least. So many passersby look angry or worried or just vacant. Occasionally your eyes catch sight of someone who seems to have a happy secret. They seem to be saying, "I know something you ought to know"—like maybe the location of a buried treasure. Any time they choose to, they can go dig it up. Perhaps they actually know the truth Paul imparted in the fourth chapter of Philippians: "And my God will meet all your needs according to his glorious riches in Christ Jesus" (v. 19). We are not poverty-stricken. There is a limitless treasure at our disposal and the awareness of that treasure is our source of joy.

Wealth is such a relative matter. If you want less than you have, you feel rich. On the other hand, even if you have great wealth, you are poor if you want more. There's another dimension to my little sidewalk game. Suppose you were suddenly accosted on the street by someone who had taken your picture surreptitiously, perhaps with a hidden camera. You have a chance to observe your own gait and expression. What does your face say to the world? What message is in your eyes? I'd like to think that I'd be walking down the street as though I knew the secret—that God would supply my every need—but I'm not sure that would be true.

I made my initial commitment to Christ in Stuttgart, Germany, just after World War II. I came home shortly afterward, and I can still remember walking the streets of Chicago, sometimes on the way to church, Fourth Presbyterian.

That congregation was located in the middle of a seamy district, not just poor but with all kinds of strip joints and seedy bars. I remember walking along and being acutely aware of the many people who seemed to be drowning in a sea of loneliness and meaninglessness. As for me, I felt as though I was surrounded by a warm cone of light coming down directly from heaven. I found myself wanting to stop strangers and say, "Listen, you're walking under water. I'm a diver, and I know where the air hose is." That's all basic evangelism is—saying, "Do you want to breathe under water? I'll tell you how."

The source of this joy that Paul repeatedly claims we should have has nothing to do with having our problems all solved or pretending we do and wearing a silly grin. In Philippians 3, Paul said, "Not that I have already obtained all this, or have already been made perfect" (v. 12). He was not what he was going to be. He hadn't yet arrived, but he could point us clearly to the holy living we want so much to attain.

Bernard Siegl is head of surgery in the Clinical Department at Yale University. He started something called "The Exceptional Cancer Patients' Therapy and Healing Program." In a talk entitled, "Love, Medicine and Miracles," he discussed the dangers of performing simply for the benefit of others—on display, grinning a lot, and trying to please. He said that cancer patients who tend to get well are the ones who do a lot of grumbling and complaining. Those who don't recover tend to be the ones who always answer, "Fine," when asked, "How are you?" or "nothing," when asked, "What's wrong?" Those patients are not dealing with reality. There's much more hope for the "difficult" patient, those who say, "I'm not getting enough attention. I want to get out of here." They are sending their immune system a message. They want to live, according to Siegl.

Paul is calling us to a joy based on the reality of our faith in God and his resources, not on pleasant circumstances or a denial of difficulties. Beverly Sills, the opera star, has said, "I'm not happy. I'm cheerful. There's a difference. A happy woman has no cares at all. A cheerful woman has cares but has learned to deal with them." That's the joy Paul was writing about. He had concerns. He was in want sometimes; he was in prison. But he was drawing on God's resources, and therefore he had joy.

A young, pregnant woman came to see me recently, concerned about the coming baby. I think she was hoping I could tell her how to pray in order to guarantee a safe delivery and a healthy child. I said, "I can't do that. Nobody can. But I believe nobody wants that baby to be well more than the Lord. He's with you. Whatever happens in this circumstance, or any other, you know the Lord, and you can rejoice in that." As we all know, bad things do happen to good people, and our joy rests in something or someone beyond our circumstances. We can say, "God is here, and I know things could be worse." As someone has said, "Even if your hair falls out, things could be worse. It could ache and have to be pulled."

Paul calls us to joy that is not based on denial. We can be realistic about our problems and say, "It's serious but I can handle this. I can move on."

In his book about General Lee, Charles Flood tells about a wonderful postwar incident. Lee, a great Christian gentleman, was visiting in the home of a woman whose house had been ravaged by Union troops during the conflict. She took her guest outside to see a particular tree. "General Lee," she said, "this beautiful, old tree was destroyed by federal cannon balls. Branches knocked off, the trunk smashed. What do you say to that?" She was expecting that he would commiserate and agree that the federal troops had acted reprehensibly. Instead, after a long pause, he said, "Cut it down, my dear madame, and forget it." We all need to do that if we are to have the joy Paul calls us to. We've all had bad things happen to us. Forget them. Move on. Don't dwell on the hurts of the past. There is a great heritage ahead.

The Honorable Max Clelland is currently the secretary of state for Georgia. Clelland was born in a Christian home, raised in a Christian church, and has given his heart to Jesus. An athlete in high school and college, he volunteered to serve in the army during the Vietnam war. He was an infantry lieutenant, and when a hand grenade was tossed in among his men, he intercepted it and tried to throw it elsewhere. But the thing that's not supposed to happen to Christians happened. The grenade exploded and blew off both his legs and one arm. I recently heard him give a moving speech in which, like Paul, he called us to rejoice, reaffirming that as Christians, nothing will ever happen to us that we can't handle.

Even death cannot end our joy. Paul wrote that to go on living means fruitful labor, but to die is also gain. "I desire to depart and be with Christ" (1:23). Ben Franklin penned these words about his eventual death:

The Body
of
Benjamin Franklin, Printer
Like the cover of an old book,
its contents torn out
And stript of its lettering and gilding,
lies food for worms.
Yet the work itself shall not be lost,
For it will (as he believed)
Appear once more

In a new
And more beautiful edition
corrected and amended
by
THE AUTHOR

There's an old Indian saying that "When you are born, you cry, and the world rejoices. May you so live that when you die, the world cries and you rejoice."

If the source of our joy is Christ and his indwelling presence, the product of joy is peace. I recently saw a bumper sticker proclaiming that "Happiness is an inside job," and it certainly is. "Rejoice," says Paul. "I will say it again: Rejoice!" Rejoice whether you have a lot or a little. It's no fun to have little, and many of us have been there. It's hard to find that comfortable middle ground. Either we have too much or we have too little. Can you enjoy too much and therefore give some of it away? Can you enjoy too little but have faith that God will provide? There are Christians who feel guilty about having enough, let alone too much. I think they miss the point. We may suffer great want at some time in life, but, in the meantime, if you have enough to eat, warm clothes, and adequate housing, enjoy it all. Praise God and share it with those who don't.

A few years back, Hazel and I received a Christmas card from a dear, old friend. The card said, "I'm not going to send you a present this year. I think most Christians already have too much." He went on to say that he was sending the amount he would have spent to a certain charity. I was put off by all that piety. I faithfully support the cause he named, but I don't plan to lay that kind of guilt trip on my friends. Why couldn't he have settled for, "I love you. Merry Christmas"? There is no shortage of people who want to make you feel guilty because you have enough. Paul had a reassuring word: "I know what it is to be in need, and I know what it is to have plenty" (4:12). He praised God in both, and so can we.

Gary Demarest, a Presbyterian pastor in California and an old friend, tells about watching a USC football game. USC is, incidentally, his alma mater. In the last few seconds, near the goal line and with one play left, USC called a time-out. The press picked up the fact that when the quarterback ran over to see the coach, they both began to laugh uproariously. The quarterback came back, and they ran the play. The press wanted to know what had so amused the two men. It seems the coach had called the quarterback over simply to say, "If you play football, you've got to enjoy this kind of thing!"

If you want to enjoy the Christian life (the most exciting game there is and one played for the highest stakes of all), you've got to learn to enjoy the hard things along with the good things. Rejoice. I will say it again: Rejoice! That's holy living.

9

Dialog:
Jesus Prays for Us

Essential to any serious attempt at holy living is, of course, prayer. Prayer is central to the whole biblical narrative and was practiced by all the men and women of faith we read about in Scripture. Prayer is implicit—and frequently explicit—on almost every page of the Bible. We can't be God's people unless we are praying people. And, in Alfred Lord Tennyson's famous words, "More things are wrought by prayer than this world dreams of."

The psalmist wrote, "Evening, morning, and noon I cry out . . ." (55:17). In the book of Daniel, we find that young man kneeling for prayer three times every day. Prayer was an integral part of his life. We read in the third chapter of Acts that Peter and John were going up to the temple at the time of prayer, three o'clock in the afternoon. They observed a regular prayer time each day.

In Acts 10 we read how two men were observing a time of prayer on the same afternoon and God was able to connect them. Cornelius, a Roman centurion and the first Gentile convert, prayed to God regularly. On this particular day, at about three o'clock in the afternoon, he had a vision. Meanwhile, in another city, the apostle Peter "went up on the roof to pray" about noon (v. 9). Both men were keeping their appointment with God, and at that time God gave Peter a message about Cornelius and directed Cornelius to send for Peter. That was how the Christian mission among Gentiles was born.

The apostle Paul made hundreds of references to prayer in his New Testament letters. In 1 Thessalonians 5 he admonishes us to "be joyful always; pray continually; give thanks in all circumstances, for this is God's will for you in Christ Jesus" (vv. 16-17).

In spite of all this, it seems it's easy to forget the centrality of prayer. Too often we are like the overweight, middle-aged businessman I saw depicted in a cartoon who knelt by his bed and began his prayers by saying, "You probably don't remember me. . . ." God's people are those who are keeping their appointment with him regularly and need not worry about being remembered.

St. Francis of Assisi frequently spent the entire night praying, often repeating just one phrase: "My God and my all, my God and my all." His relationship with God was a love affair. Martin Luther, a more earthy type, said, "No one knows how strong and mighty prayer is, and how much it can do, except he . . . who has tried it." Horace Bushnell, who was one of our nation's premier Christian educators, put it this way: "I fell into the habit of talking to God, and do it now without knowing." That's prayer—sometimes, in the watches of the night, it's pillow talk. Sometimes we pray on the run, while driving down the highway or walking along the street, saying repeatedly, "Lord, thank you. Lord, help me. Lord, bless that needy person."

Dr. Alexis Carrell, a pioneer in wholistic medicine, wrote, "Prayer is a force as real as terrestrial gravitation. As a physician, I have seen men, after all their therapy failed, lifted out of disease and melancholy by the serene effort of prayer." T. S. Eliot wrote, "Life is just our chance to learn to pray." It would follow then that if we don't learn to pray we've wasted our life.

Dr. Paul Chu is pastor of the world's largest congregation, in Seoul, Korea. American pastors often ask him to tell them the secret of such church growth because they want to know how their churches can experience the same moving of God. In reply to those kinds of questions he writes, "How many times have you spent all night on your knees before God? How often has your church called all of its members together for prolonged fasting and prayer? Could this be the reason you are not experiencing revival in your life and ministry?"

Another word about prayer comes from an unlikely source: the late actor Cary Grant: "If you don't have faith, pray anyway. If you don't understand or believe the words you're saying, pray anyway. Prayer can start faith, particularly if you pray aloud. And even the most imperfect prayer is an attempt to reach God."

Each February our nation celebrates a World Day of Prayer. It's a time to join with Christians all over the country and bring our concerns before God. The custom originated with Abraham Lincoln who, on the eve of the Civil War, called for a day of national repentance through prayer. He wrote: "We have forgotten God. We have forgotten the gracious hand which preserved us in peace, and multiplied and enriched and strengthened us; and we have vainly imagined, in the deceitfulness of our hearts, that all these blessings were produced by some superior wisdom and virtue of our own. Intoxicated with unbroken success, we have become too self-sufficient to feel the necessity of redeeming and preserving grace, too proud to pray to the God that made us. It behooves us then to humble ourselves . . . to confess our national sins, and to pray for clemency and forgiveness."

Here are some guidelines for prayer to help you reinforce your relationship with the heavenly Father. To begin with, pray frequently and regularly. Pray so spontaneously that you actually forget you're praying—you're just talking to God throughout the day. Pray specifically. Jesus taught us to ask God each day for our daily bread. We need to tell God about our physical and material needs. Pray positively. Jesus told his disciples and also tells us, "Whatever you ask for in prayer, believe that you have received it, and it will be yours" (Mark 11:24). If you're praying for a friend who is sick or disabled or suffering from depression, don't picture the illness. Instead, visualize that organ well, that bone healed, that melancholy lifted. Imagine your friend dancing and laughing before the Lord and claim that as fact, saying, "Lord, I know that's what you want." Pray informally as well as formally—alone, in small groups, or in great congregations where prayers of confession and for the needs of your parish, the nation, and the world are lifted during worship.

We have said that prayer is central to the Christian life, but we need to keep in mind that prayer is dialog. It is a two-way conversation. In prayer you are talking to someone else—your Father, Creator, Redeemer, and Friend. I'm sure you have occasionally had the unhappy experience of being trapped for a whole evening with someone who seems to have zero interest in you. They may have fed you, and so you feel some sense of obligation, but you know there will be no reprieve until the evening ends. They simply want to tell you all about their faith, their political views, their latest vacation, their kids, and their grandkids. You are a captive audience, and you sit and listen as graciously as you can until it is reasonable to announce that you have to go. Let's face it, it is *boring* to be with people for whom you are an audience, an audience who needs only to nod occasionally. In any good relationship, the conversation is like a game of Ping-Pong. The ball bounces back and forth.

One of my favorite movies is an old one entitled, "The Wrong Box." The hero, if we can call him that, is a man who knows something about everything. He is a fountain of trivia. In one scene he is traveling in a railroad coach, and the other passengers have no means of escape. "Do you know," he queries, "how many times the word *work* is used in the Bible? Three hundred and twenty-two (or some such number)," and the monolog is launched. We are not to behave like that in our prayer life.

If we are talking to God, we ought to, out of courtesy, begin to listen to him as well. We need a time of quiet when God can talk to *us*, and if we take that time seriously enough, we will have a notebook and pencil at hand to write down the things that come to mind—a name, a specific task to undertake. Write it all down. If you follow up on those visions, you will more often than not find God has been speaking to you.

My life was changed irrevocably years ago by a man who listened to God. I was a first-year student in seminary at the time. George Morrison was a senior, and considered by the rest of us an old man—almost 30. Like me, he had met Jesus Christ during the war years. He had been serving in the army in Egypt and was converted there by some American missionaries. After seminary he returned to Egypt as a missionary himself. He was two years ahead of me in seminary and belonged to a different eating club, so we were barely acquainted. George had been serving as a minister in a little church up on the Hudson River. He began to pray about who should replace him and serve this tiny congregation when he graduated. He claims that God clearly gave him my name. One day in chapel he approached me with the idea. "George," I said, "I have plans for the summer. I'm going overseas, and I have no interest in that little church." "Will you pray about it?" he asked. Grudgingly, I agreed. Oddly enough, there were three students in his own eating club hounding him for that job. "Put my name in, George. I need the money." George was steadfast. "God told me Bruce Larson is to go there."

Eventually his stubbornness wore me out. I prayed long and hard and finally agreed to go. You're waiting to hear that revival broke out in that parish as a result, right? Not by a long shot. However, I did meet my wife in that little church, and there is no way in the world we'd have met if somebody hadn't been listening to God. There's nothing logical about what George claimed was God's clear guidance. That's the kind of openended adventure we're in for as we listen to God. When we pay attention to what he's saying, God can change our lives and even somebody else's.

There's a story I love about Henry B. Wright, who was a brilliant professor at Yale University. He had become a devout Christian, and one day he learned that a former classmate was on skid row, a wino, hanging out in New York's Bowery District. Distressed by this bad news, Wright looked him up, and soon was making regular trips to New York to visit him. But he seemed unable to motivate his friend to change his destructive habits. One day, after one of those discouraging visits, he was returning by train to New Haven and reading his Bible when God seemed to speak to him: "Henry, buy him a gold watch. Put this inscription on the back: 'To John with best regards from Henry.'" Wright thought this was unusual guidance, especially on a professor's salary, but he did it. He bought a watch and had it inscribed, and the following week he went in to town to present it to his friend. That extravagant gift so moved his friend that he never again touched a drop of liquor. That tangible evidence of Wright's love and concern helped his old classmate to walk away from a life of alcoholism. Flushed with victory, Wright tried this strategy a second time with another acquaintance who had become a drunken vagrant. The second man promptly sold the watch and bought a bottle of booze. The point came home to Henry B. Wright. There is no one strategy for reaching with two different people. God's guidance is unique for each situation.

Having said that prayer is and must be dialog, what about the other side of prayer? What is Jesus praying about concerning us? Are you aware that right now he is praying for us to the Father, calling us by name and petitioning for John—Helen—Mary—Bill?

What exactly is Jesus praying? The 17th chapter of John's gospel reports that at three different times Jesus said, "I pray" or "I am praying." Jesus did not say he *had been* praying or *did* pray, but "I am praying." And we can trust that Jesus continues to pray to the Father for us. Whatever else he is praying for, one prayer is that we "may be one." He is praying that we might be reconciled with all of those with whom we are not one right now. It is staggering to realize that not only can Jesus answer our prayers, but that we can answer his prayers for us. We are answering those prayers whenever we move toward reconciliation with another member of his family.

Whatever else Satan is up to in this sinful world, we know he is the author of discord and enmity. His strategy is to divide and separate. In his book *The Great Divorce*, C. S. Lewis portrayed hell as a place where people are continually moving farther and farther away from each other, where they abhor community and close relationships. The letter to the Ephesians is a call to oneness but that does not mean we merge into one big blob of Jell-O. Each of us is to become more and more distinct while, at the same time, we move closer and closer in love and harmony.

Alexis de Tocqueville, that insightful Frenchman who wrote about America in the 1830s, saw the problem. He described it in sociological terms. "In democracies where the members of the community never differ much from each other and naturally stand so near that they may at any time be fused in one general mass, numerous artificial and arbitrary distinctions spring up by means of which every man hopes to keep himself aloof lest he should be carried away against his will into the crowd. This can never fail to be the case, for human institutions can be changed, but man cannot, whatever may be the general endeavor of a community to render its members equal and alike, the personal pride of individuals will always be to rise above the line and to form an inequality to their own advantage."

Jesus' prayer that we might be one is crucial on all sorts of levels. Week by week as I counsel parents, children, and spouses, I'm all too aware of the need for oneness within our family structures. Infidelity is a major problem. One member of a marriage has been unfaithful and the other is wounded to the heart, as they should be. Divorce often seems the only logical next step. What a miracle when the one who has been unfaithful can repent of that sin and the injured party can say, "It was a terrible betrayal and the scar will always be there, but nevertheless, we are one. With God's help, I'm going to forgive as I am forgiven." That doesn't always happen, but when it does, it's nothing short of a miracle, and it is the kind of reconciliation Jesus is praying will happen.

Phyllis Diller says, "Never go to bed mad. Stay up and

fight." But whether we go to bed mad or stay up and fight, we need to work toward reconciliation. We might even remind our partner, "Jesus is praying, darling, that you and I might be one."

Jesus is also praying that the church might be one. Many of us would like to make the church over into our own image. Why can't we be of one mind about all those controversial issues—abortion, the arms race, our policies in Central America, to name a few. As a church we are tragically divided, both theologically and on social issues. Yet we are committed to loving our Christian brothers and sisters—whether they share our point of view or not—and to work toward reconciliation. Jesus is praying that we will succeed.

In *The History of Missions,* M. M. Thomas, an Indian Christian, wrote about the breakdown of the caste system. It seems that when the early missionaries came to India, their converts were, for the first time, required to gather around the communion table together, regardless of caste. Those of high caste were expected to come to the table with the pariahs, the outcasts. At first they refused. "No way. We will accept Jesus as our Savior, but we will not accept our outcast brothers at this table." They were told they could not accept Jesus as Savior without accepting all Christians as brothers and sisters, regardless of caste. This was very painful, but finally they understood the rightness of it. Soon, comingling at the sacrament became commonplace, but they still wouldn't fraternize socially. While high-caste Christians would come to the Lord's table with the outcasts, they were certainly not about to take afternoon tea with them. Finally, even that barrier broke down. They are now one, as Jesus has prayed they would be, without caste divisions.

Jesus is praying that you will be one with your enemies. How do you deal with those people who are out to get you, or have already gotten you? Is reconciliation a possibility? Festo Kivengere, the well-known Ugandan bishop, tells about an incident that occurred during a recent preaching mission in his country. In the middle of the sermon, a young man who had just arrived from Zaire went forward and knelt at the altar. The bishop asked the reason for this unusual interruption. "Today is a great day for me," said the man. "I am out of my prison! Four years ago the rebels in my country, people in our own village, took my mother and father and murdered them in cold blood in front of me. I decided I would never forgive them at all. Immediately I entered into the prison of an unforgiving spirit. But as you brothers were speaking, I heard the voice from Calvary, 'Father, forgive them for they don't know what they are doing' (Luke 23:34). The door to my cell fell wide open as God's forgiving love entered my heart. Now I want to go back and share with those men who murdered my parents how much God loves them in Jesus Christ." We have only one option in dealing with our enemies. We forgive them and we love them. This young African not only did that, he went on to evangelize them.

Sometimes we need to be reconciled not with our enemies, but with our friends—the brother or sister in your prayer group, the fellow member of the missions committee. Sometimes it is a close friend or family member who has really hurt us. I received a letter a while back from a woman who, with her husband, had been in my office for counseling. It said, in part, "Yesterday, after you got us together and made us forgive each other and left us, I knew I had to 'do what was expected and right.' My husband and I went through the motions of asking each others' forgiveness and hugging, but I was absolutely dead inside. Then I remembered something you said. You were talking about dealing with depression and you said that long years of analysis were not necessary; if we could just pretend we felt the way we should, the feelings would eventually come. Anyway, I went home totally exhausted, having pretended that I forgave him and cried myself to sleep. When I wakened a few hours later, the feelings were there—the right ones—I was able to say, 'I did a stupid thing' and own it. Then followed a wonderful time of closeness with the Lord. . . . Incredibly, this all makes sense to me, though it may not make any sense whatsoever to you on this paper."

It makes sense to me, and I'm sure it does to you. We've all been hurt, and we know how hard it is to say, "I was wrong. I love you. I need you. Forgive me." But those are the steps we need to take if we are to honor the prayer Jesus tells us he is making on our behalf. He is our Savior. We can bring him our problems and burdens, but he wants us to be aware that he is praying for us. We have the power to be an answer to his prayers whenever we move toward reconciliation with a family member, a Christian brother or sister, an enemy or a friend. Jesus prayed and is praying that we might be one. At the heart of holy living is reconciliation.

10

Dialog:
What, Where, and Why

Many years ago the American novelist Sinclair Lewis addressed a group of writing classes at New York University. Before he began his talk, he asked his sizable audience, "How many of you intend to earn a living at writing?" About half the hands went up. "In that case," said the author, "Why don't you go home and start writing? I'll talk to the others." If you are going to make a living by writing, you start by writing, and you write and keep on writing. You don't just go to classes on writing.

I'm just as convinced that if you are going to learn to pray, you start by praying, and you pray and keep on praying. I'm not sure there's much help to be found in sermons on prayer or workshops on prayer or books on prayer. In this mysterious, powerful dialog with our Creator, we're all students in the school of prayer, and we can only learn by doing.

At an annual retreat in our congregation, one of our pastoral staff members was asked to speak to us about prayer. He said, "You know, my brothers and sisters, I don't know much about prayer, and I find prayer very difficult. That's why I pray so often with everybody I can. I need practice." For those of us who feel called to holy living, prayer is something we can't practice often enough. To that end, I want to explore with you some of the hows and wheres and whys of prayer, with the hope that they will motivate all of us to practice more often.

The best-known and most universally used prayer is, of course, the Lord's Prayer. Some years ago I was studying the 11th chapter of Luke and the circumstances under which Jesus gave his followers that famous prayer. Pondering those verses, it seemed to me that something didn't ring true. Let's remember that Jesus was a Jew, not a Greek. If you asked a Greek to teach you his philosophy, he'd say, "Come to my classroom or workshop, bring your notebook, and I'll teach you all about it." If you asked a Jew that question, he'd say, "Come and live with me. Observe who I am and what I do." Jesus was part of that tradition. He took 12 people to live with him for three years. He didn't begin their training by teaching them to pray. Rather, after some time together, they perceived that prayer was an important part of his life and they said, "Lord, teach us to pray."

We can understand why the disciples would be motivated to ask that question; nevertheless, the prayer we read about that Jesus gave them seems so uncharacteristic of him. I do not see Jesus as someone who would suggest that this part of our devotional life be done by rote, or at least not most of the time. I have misgivings about the fact that weekly, in congregations across this land, we pray that same prayer word for word, as if they were the only possible and efficacious words. My conviction is that the prayer we find in

Luke 11 is actually an outline of what our prayers ought to include, and not a mandate to repeat those same, exact words to express those thoughts and needs.

I have adapted that prayer in my own private devotions to a slightly different form. First of all, I pray in pictures. The best communication does not necessarily require words. In the prayer our Lord gave his disciples, there are six, clear, distinct pictures. I remember those six pictures by using the letters CHRIST, which form, of course, our Lord's own title. Let's try an experiment, and let's pray the Lord's prayer in terms of the pictures that this acrostic conjures up.

"C" is for concentrate. Concentrate on and picture God. Where do you think this Creator God is? The picture Jesus supplied is conveyed by, "Our Father *in heaven.*" Where exactly is that? Is it a place outside the cosmos, from which God caused this great, expanding bang which created the universe of which the earth is just a tiny part? Or does God encompass all? The cosmos may exist inside the body of God. We are all part of God's body, a body bigger than the cosmos. Perhaps God "in heaven" exists in some timeless dimension in which we are some little adjunct. But "C" reminds us to *concentrate* on where God is. We can't see God's face. No one has seen God's face in this world. But think of the place where you picture God, and picture God there right now.

The letter "H" moves us to the second picture. *"H" is for hallelujah* and represents an attitude of praise and wonder and thanksgiving to God, wherever you picture him. When you say, "Father," you immediately have access to God. You can picture yourself having his attention, his concern. Picture God wanting to talk to you and eager to listen to you. It's a picture that makes the heart well up with praise and wonder: "Hallelujah, holy, holy, holy. Thank you, Jesus; thank you, Father; thank you, Holy Spirit."

The letter "R" is for ruler. We know that God the Creator, Jesus the Lord, and the Holy Spirit, this triune God, is the ruler of all. But our little planet is still caught in the struggle between good and evil. There is a battle going on here between God, the ruler of everything, and the adversary, the prince of darkness. In this picture see yourself enlisting in God's holy army, saying, "Lord, I want to sign up. Where do I enlist? I want to be part of your army, someone through whom you can work to bring your rule to this world."

"I" is my code for two phrases—"I need" and "I feed." Picture those things you need most right now (daily bread, a job, reconciliation, money, healing). Complete that "I need . . . " sentence with a picture: "I need a friend" . . . "I need to be healed in a relationship" . . . "I need hope." Be specific and picture that need in your mind. Then say, "I feed." Picture God supplying that which you need. Believe that you have it and you will receive it. That's the promise we have. Picture what you need, visualize God providing it, and say, "Thank you."

The "S" of our acrostic is for sin. Picture in your mind the thing for which you are most ashamed right now. If you're not ashamed of anything, you ought to be. We're all sinners. Try to picture that person you have hurt, that moral waivering, that dishonesty, that cowardice, that unloving word. Try to picture it all clearly, and then picture Jesus saying, as he did from the cross, "Father, forgive them" (Luke 23:34). "If we confess our sins, he is faithful and just and will forgive us our sins . . ." (1 John 1:9).

The letter for the final picture, "T," is for temptation. Picture your present temptations. Are you tempted to take your future into your own hands—to provide for your own needs—financial, sexual, vocational—apart from God's will? Are you tempted to be something you're not? To put somebody down? To cheat? Picture that specific temptation, and then picture the Lord putting his hand out. Put your hand in his and say, "Lead me away from that. I trust you. Thank you. Praise your name. Amen." As I have been praying the Lord's Prayer by using these kinds of pictures over the past four years, it has been a transforming experience for me. I hope it will be useful for you as well.

That's just one "how" of prayer as we think about the Lord's Prayer. Let's move on now to the "where" of prayer, using Jesus as our model. In Matthew 6:6 he says, "When you pray, go into your room, close the door and pray to your Father, who is unseen. Then your Father, who sees what is done in secret, will reward you." Our prayer life should include a time alone when, armed with our Bible and perhaps a notebook and pencil, we say, "Lord, it's just you and me for the next minutes." As I said earlier, write down those ideas that come to mind. They might very well be God's leading for you. Sometimes God's guidance seems puzzling. But as we continue to seek him, he reveals more of his will. We may never fully understand, but we have a Father who speaks to us, who gives us, bit by bit, light for the journey. We are never given so much light that we outgrow our need for him.

But we don't do all our praying alone. In Mark 14 we read, "They went to a place called Gethsemane, and Jesus said to his disciples, 'Sit here while I pray.' He took Peter, James and John along with him, and he began to be deeply distressed and troubled" (vv. 32-33). When we are greatly distressed and troubled, we may need other believers around us. In those times we don't go into our closet alone. We say, as Jesus did, "I am greatly distressed. Sit with me. Watch with me. Pray with me."

Dietrich Bonhoeffer once wrote, "Let him who cannot

be alone beware of community. . . . Let him who is not in community beware of being alone. . . . Each by itself has profound pitfalls and perils. One who wants fellowship without solitude plunges into the void of words and feelings, and one who seeks solitude without fellowship perishes in the abyss of vanity, self-infatuation, and despair." That is a good corrective for our prayer life. Each of us is more comfortable in one or the other of those circumstances— praying alone or praying in small or large groups. Bonhoeffer wisely counseled us to do whichever is the least comfortable.

In the 17th chapter of John, we find Jesus praying with a larger group, all 12 disciples—another "where" of prayer. Picture the 13 of them around the table. How do you think Jesus began the lengthy prayers recorded on that occasion? Do you think he said, "Now please stop eating. Put your knives and forks down. Fold your hands and bow your heads. I'm going to pray for us all"? I'm certain it happened more naturally and spontaneously than that. Nowhere in the Bible does it say that we are required to bow our heads and close our eyes when we pray. Why not pray looking at the faces of our brothers and sisters, thanking God for them and asking his blessing on them and praying—as I'd like to think Jesus might have done in the upper room—open-eyed prayers?

The Gospels tell us further that Jesus prayed in church, or, actually, in the synagogue. In Mark 1 we find him going to the synagogue and taking part in corporate prayer. He also prayed on the road. That's a good place to pray. Two of the gospel writers tell about a curious incident that took place on the road. Jesus was hungry, and as he walked along, he spied a fig tree in full bloom. Examining it more closely, there was not a single fig to be found. His prayer was that the unproductive tree be cursed. It withered and died within a day's time.

I find that story somewhat comforting. Many of us have been exasperated enough on the highway to want to curse somebody. A friend of mind tells about being on an entrance ramp to our local freeway, where a sign instructs drivers to "yield." He got behind somebody who just kept waiting and waiting as traffic roared by. Exasperated, my friend rolled down his window and yelled, "The sign says, 'yield,' not 'give up'!" Pray for people who cut you off on the highway. Pray for careless pedestrians. Make God a part of even that mundane part of your day, driving down the freeway or walking down Main Street. They're both great times for prayer.

Jesus said grace before meals—another "where" of prayer. When they brought him the loaves and the fishes, Jesus said grace over meager rations and look what happened. I've never been embarrassed about saying grace in a restaurant since I returned home from the war in Germany. During the occupation, I watched old people and little children going through those big GI garbage cans into which we had scraped the leavings from our mess kits. Some soggy bread or some tiny piece of fat or gristle would be taken home to share. The conquering army had plenty and the civilians had nothing. Having enough to eat was not something to be taken for granted.

In the world today, those just as deserving as we have empty bellies. We know about them and we try to help. But just having enough to eat is an enormous blessing in this unfair world. Don't be embarrassed to say, "Lord, I want to thank you. It's undeserved, but thank you." And if you are embarrassed to do that in a public place, use an open-eyed grace. Praying before meals, both public and private, is a basic part of a life of prayer.

In Matthew 19 we find Jesus praying with children. "Then little children were brought to Jesus for him to place his hands on them and pray for them" (v. 13). The disciples tried to discourage them, saying, "He's too busy," but Jesus rebuked them. I hope you're not too busy to pray with your children. It is one time when parent and child are equally needy and vulnerable before the Lord. The reality of your faith will be communicated in those times of prayer more effectively than by almost any other means.

Jesus prayed for those who were sick, and they were healed. In Luke 11 he goes into a home where a little girl had just died. All the relatives and neighbors were weeping and mourning. Jesus arrived on the scene with reassurances that she would be all right. They laughed at him. In order to restore her, Jesus had to perform a "doubtectomy." He asked all the people who were weeping and mourning, all those who mocked and laughed, to leave the scene. They were a block to God's healing. He took the parents, who held onto a hope born of despair, and three of the disciples and went into the room where the little girl lay. He brought in a faith climate—a group of believers. Often those who are ill are surrounded by doubters, however well-meaning. If we go to pray for their healing, we need to do what Jesus did here. Ask the doubters to leave, and bring two or three believers along to pray. That's the climate of faith that allows God's healing Spirit to work.

Jesus lamented for Jerusalem and must have prayed for that city many times. Perhaps you have stood, as I have, on that high hill looking over Jerusalem, with the Kidron Valley below. It's so moving to think of Jesus standing in that place and interceding for the people and the pain of that city. He had spent enough time there to have great insight about the problems and sins of the people of Jerusalem—not just the beggars and lepers, but also the fat cats in business and government who thought they had it made, those with broken marriages, vices and addictions, those who practiced exploitation and corruption. During that last triumphal entry, Jesus wept over the city, saying, "If you, even you, had only known on this day what would bring you peace . . ." (Luke 19:42).

I hope you pray for your city, town, or village. In Seattle, the view from a place like the Space Needle is spectacular. But even in our beautiful city it is immediately apparent that pain and sin are not at all confined to the districts where winos or street people hang out. They are everywhere, at every level of life. We need to pray about being a light and leaven that will bless the people of our city.

Finally, our Lord prayed in the marketplace, in the midst of the hubbub of life. Even on the cross, he prayed for all the people milling around below, soldiers as well as spectators. He prayed, "Father, forgive them, for they do not know what they are doing" (Luke 23:34). There are times when we feel we are being crucified, used, manipulated, or dumped on. Those are good times to pray. Jesus modeled how to do that. Don't pretend it feels good, but ask God to bless all the people involved, even your persecutors. Our marketplace includes all the busyness of life, where from time to time we will be crucified by indifference or rejection, by chicanery or betrayal.

A man told me recently about finding a way to pray in the business world. "I promised to pray for somebody with a serious problem a while back," he said, "every day for 30 days. I'm not that faithful in prayer, and I was afraid I'd forget. I came up with a plan. I'm a computer programmer and I start every day with a log-in, at least 30 seconds when the machine is warming up. I pasted the prayer on the terminal and used that time to pray for my friend. At first it was only 30 seconds a day, but eventually I was praying long after the screen came on, sometimes four or five minutes. Those 30 days brought miracles in my friend's life, and now that's my regular prayer time. There's a new request pasted up every month." This friend found a way to be reminded to pray in those busy times and places in the marketplace of his life.

But perhaps the essential question is not where to pray, but why? Primarily we pray to praise God and to be in relationship with him. In 1 Thessalonians Paul wrote, "Be joyful always; pray continually; give thanks in all circumstances, for this is God's will for you in Christ Jesus." As we pray in all of those circumstances, we are affirming that God is, that he is with us, and that he is sovereign in everything that's going on right now in your life or mine. We don't praise him for the painful things—those crucifixions we mentioned earlier—but we praise a God powerful enough to raise Jesus from the dead, who is able to raise us from whatever pit we are in.

The third verse of Psalm 22 says God is "enthroned on the praises of Israel." When you and I praise God in all things wherever we are, alone or in a group, at meals or on the highway, with children or with the sick and bereaved or in the marketplace, power is released. The places of prayer are everywhere. As we pray without ceasing, giving thanks in all things, God works through our prayers to bring about his will in our lives, in the lives of friends and family, in our cities, and in the world. At the center of our call to holy living is the daily dialog of prayer.

11

A Peacemaker's Dialog

Those of us who are faithful, praying Christians have all kinds of evidence that our specific prayers are and have been answered. We have seen relationships mended, bodies healed, directions changed. In fact, we could catalog many events and circumstances explainable only by divine intervention of a personal God in our personal lives. Yet even with all that evidence, it is difficult to believe that our prayers could change the course of history or the world, things so outside the realm of our involvement and control.

All of this brings us to the matter of prayers for peace. In small and large companies, and in churches and cathedrals across the world, prayers for peace have been offered by generations of faithful, individual believers. In our own time of global unrest, wars, terrorism, and oppression, there are few questions more pertinent than the relevancy and efficacy of our continued prayers for peace.

Dr. Albert Einstein, my old neighbor at Princeton, was

asked just before he died, "What kind of weapons do you think they will be using in World War III?" "I don't know," was the reply, "but I do know what weapons will be used if there is ever a World War IV. Rocks! Definitely rocks." He understood, as few people would, the terrible price to be paid should our peace efforts fail. Jesus said to that crowd on the mountain at Galilee, "Blessed are the peacemakers, for they will be called sons of God" (Matt. 5:9). It seems, then, that if we are to be the sons (and daughters) of God, we have no other course than to work for peace and to pray for peace.

But the New Testament narrative presents us with some contradictions in terms of peacemaking. The word *peacemaker*, which Matthew records from the Sermon on the Mount and which has become so common in our time, is used only once in the Bible. And in Luke 22:36 we find these strange words, again spoken by Jesus: "But now if you have a purse, take it, and also a bag, and if you don't have a sword, sell your cloak and buy one." And in Matthew 10:34-36 Jesus is quoted as saying, "Do not suppose that I have come to bring peace to the earth. I did not come to bring peace, but a sword. For I have come to turn 'a man against his father, a daughter against her mother, a daughter-in-law against her mother-in-law." There are a good many Christians who have firsthand experience of the truth of those words. Their Christian commitment and their attempts to take that commitment seriously have resulted in estrangement, sometimes even enmity, with other family members who neither support nor understand their new way of life.

When the angels announced the birth of our Lord they talked about peace: "Glory to God in the highest, and on earth peace to men on whom his favor rests" (Luke 2:14). Unfortunately, there is no promise there of universal peace.

If we look to the Bible for a clear message about peace, it is not to be found.

It seems the world is just as confused on the issue. Our nation's capitol is full of peace monuments, a new one erected after each war. From a secular point of view, I suppose peace would be defined as the cessation of war or hostilities. That kind of peace between nations is certainly a possibility, and it's a kind of peace we have enjoyed many times in history. The *Pax Romana* is perhaps the most famous example. The Romans conquered the whole known world and their enemies ceased to resist. "Peace" prevailed. Only a century ago, we had a Peace Britannica. Britannia ruled the waves and Britain's empire extended all over the globe, and there was peace. We could have peace today. All we need to do is submit to our enemies, to the Soviet Union or whomever, and let them occupy and rule our land. Then we would enjoy "peace."

But assuming our nation could negotiate some kind of peace with all our enemies, we would still need to make peace between the divided interests and factions within. The fabric of our national life is slashed into so many different pieces, all with conflicting interests. When President Reagan came into office the air traffic controllers were at war with the government, on strike for more wages and better conditions. Now we have peace. The two groups could not reconcile their differences. Peace resulted when one of those groups was eliminated.

Again, if we are defining peace as the cessation of hostilities, then it is always attainable, even in families. The TV antihero Archie Bunker is our model. When he laid down the law, everybody trembled and there was peace in the Bunker family. It's a caricature, of course, but we all know families in which one person is the authority, imposing his or her will on the other members. Peace prevails, but bought at the expense of another's personhood and autonomy.

Inner peace is also possible through the cessation of hostilities, according to the secular world. We are presented with all sorts of avenues to that sort of peace. We can be like Cheech and Chong, floating through life, mellow and high, with no inner conflicts. Alcohol or drugs are a route to this kind of inner peace. You can become a Hare Krishna and wear a robe and chant mindlessly, and all of your problems leave, or so they tell us. You can put yourself in the hands of a guru, or practice Scientology. Those are just some of the routes to inner peace the world offers us, in order to end the hostility inside. It's a false and pointless kind of peace.

From a purely secular point of view, it seems to me there are at least three major strategies for bringing about that cessation of hostilities we've been talking about. First of all, we can maintain peace by means of threats or intimidation. We can get our will by throwing our weight around in the office, at home, or in school. The school bully is probably the most familiar example. Some of you may still remember those awful days when some bully would be lying in wait for you outside the locker room. A few years ago, the movie *My Bodyguard* gave some of us a chance to get back at that frightening character, at least vicariously. A little, skinny kid in Chicago, having taken all the intimidation he could stand, went out and hired the biggest kid around to be his bodyguard. And how the audience cheered when the bully finally got his comeuppance!

Sometimes it's hard to tell a bully from a prophet. People with that special mixture of charisma and forcefulness can galvanize the rest of us into action, sometimes for our own good. Many outstanding leaders, past and present, have had that kind of unyielding, I-know-what's-best-for-everybody style. Those characteristics may manifest themselves early in life. I heard about a young boy who came into his town bank clutching $25 and wanting to open an account. He was asked by the teller where he got all that money. "Selling greeting cards," he answered. "You must have sold lots of cards to lots of people to make $25." "No," said the boy, "I sold them all to one family—after their dog bit me." He was one of those people who was able to make even adversity work for him, and undoubtedly on his way to being either a bully or a prophet.

A second strategy for bringing about that cessation of hostility is to be a pacifist. But if it's hard sometimes to distinguish the bully from the prophet, it's often just as hard to tell the pacifist from the wimp. Both say, "Under no circumstances will I fight. I will lay down my weapons and turn the other cheek. I will not retaliate." India's Gandhi is, of course, the patron saint of pacifists, and he did achieve significant victories using that strategy against the British. But even Gandhi supported the war against Nazi Germany in World War II. He recognized that his pacifist techniques worked only against a moral enemy. Evil or immoral enemies will simply use their opponents' pacifism to gain their own ends.

The third strategy for gaining peace, from a worldly point of view, is through negotiations. This is most operable when both sides negotiate from the position of power. At the top of the pyramid we have our president and the Soviet leader at a summit meeting. But peace through negotiation is practical at all levels, from labor/management disputes down to personal ones.

Amazingly enough, in Great Britain the slavery issue was

solved through negotiation. In our own nation, that question was resolved only after a bloody civil war. Slavery was abolished in Great Britain primarily through William Wilberforce and a few people like him who believed strongly that it was an evil practice and against God's will. Their negotiations took years and years, but abolition was achieved without the loss of a single life.

Peace through negotiations can work even in a marriage. It depends mainly on what's in your heart. When I counsel someone about his or her floundering marriage, the first question I ask is, "Do you want this marriage to work? What is in your heart? If you love this person, God will show us the strategy to make the marriage work." Negotiations will be successful only when there is a genuine desire for reconciliation and peace.

Peace is a priority for the secular world, especially in these troubled times. We honor our professional peacemakers—ambassadors, diplomats, negotiators, conciliators, judges, lawyers, psychologists, counselors, politicians, ombudsmen. We honor those who are professionally involved in peacemaking between nations and groups and individuals and those who are legitimately helping people find inner peace through counseling, psychotherapy, and similar means. As Christians, you and I need to be praying for all of those peacemakers. But let's keep in mind that biblical peace is something entirely different.

The Bible approaches this matter of peace from a radical and surprising perspective. In John 14:27 we read Jesus' words, "Peace I leave with you; my peace I give you. I do not give to you as the world gives." The Bible indicates that this peace comes from a person. That has nothing to do with the strategies for peace we've discussed so far—bullying, pacifying, negotiating. Paul wrote to the Ephesians that

Jesus "himself is our peace, who has made the two one and has destroyed the barrier, the dividing wall of hostility . . ." (2:15). Not only does peace come from a person, peace *is* a person.

It seems to me there are at least three marks of this peace the Bible promises. First, this peace that comes from and through Jesus is a peace motivated by love, not fear. Our motive for negotiating peace with the Soviets right now is fear, not love. Second, it is a costly peace. The person involved in that kind of peacemaking is required to absorb a lot of the pain of the situation. As Jesus has taken our sins and burdens upon himself, we are to love as he has loved, to pour out ourselves sacrificially and renounce our own self-interest if we are to bring about reconciliation and peace.

Third, peace from a biblical perspective is marked by its ability to *proact* rather than *react*. I mentioned William Wilberforce's role in the abolition of slavery in Britain. Every slaveholder was reimbursed by the government for his slaves. The nation absorbed the financial burden of that brave and bold, new policy. Wilberforce had been converted in college, and his entire life seemed to be filled with the glory and wonder of Jesus. His years in Parliament were devoted to freeing the British Empire from the yoke of slavery. Here's what he wrote: "I must confess equally that my own solid hopes for the well-being of my country depend, not so much on our navies and armies, nor on the wisdom of her rulers, nor on the spirit of her people, as on the persuasion that she still contains many who love and obey the Gospel of Christ. I believe that their prayers may yet prevail." Handicapped and of small stature, Wilberforce nevertheless towered over all of his contemporaries. He was convinced that his cause would succeed because of the significant few lawmakers in whom Jesus dwelt, who were praying that the slavery issue would be resolved.

I wish I did more proacting instead of the reacting that seems to come so much more readily. I get a good deal of mail, including some of those poison-pen, hate letters. My tendency is to want to ignore them, or to write back a nasty reply. I heard about a well-known man who had a system for dealing with that kind of mail. He returned those letters to the sender with this message added at the bottom. "The enclosed letter arrived on my desk a few days ago. I am sending it to you in the belief that as a responsible citizen you should know that some idiot is sending out letters over your signature. Cordially yours." That's one kind of proacting. However, a far better solution is to absorb the anger and, motivated by love, try to respond in a way that promotes reconciliation.

A Gallup poll revealed that the majority of Americans believed that Bernard Goetz acted rightly in shooting four young men who were trying to intimidate and rob him in a subway. What does that say about the mood in America? A desk sergeant on the television program, "Hill Street Blues," sent out his officers on patrol every morning with this phrase: "Do it to them before they do it to you." That is the kind of peace Mr. Goetz was establishing. He planned to carry a gun, and before those thieves and muggers could get him, he would let them have it. The majority of Americans apparently cheered for that.

Peacemaking from the biblical perspective is something radically different. Judy Lawson's story is a case in point. She is a Florida resident, the mother of six. Her oldest son was killed nine years ago, shot to death during a drug deal with a 12-gauge shotgun at point-blank range. The man who shot him, Richard Wine, and his partner were ultimately apprehended and brought to trial. Judy Lawson is a Christian, and from the time that she knew the identity of her son's murderer, she began to pray for Richard Wine. She says, "In the flesh I might have torn him limb-from-limb. But I didn't want hate, anger or revenge in my life." She felt she had a calling from God to pray for and to love Richard. She says, "I asked to see Richard through God's eyes. During the trial she got to meet Richard and tried to speak with him. Richard would have nothing to do with this woman, the mother of the man he murdered. For the next four years Judy wrote him faithfully, repeating often that Jesus loved him and so did she. Richard says he wrote back "any perverted thing I could think of."

A turning point came when Richard was put into solitary confinement, with only the Bible to read. He read it from cover to cover in 11 days. And Jesus' love and redemption burst into his life. These days, Judy drives 90 miles to the Avon Park Correctional Institute every Sunday after church. She visits her new son Richard. Judy's five remaining children still don't understand why she cares for the man who killed their brother. "I sat them down and explained that an ability to forgive came from God," Judy says. "I didn't want resentment to prevent me from seeing Richard as God saw him."

That's the peacemaking Jesus calls us to. That kind of peacemaking is absolutely impossible between natural enemies apart from God's intervention through the death and resurrection and presence of Jesus Christ. In the final analysis, that is the only kind of peacemaking that will ever resolve enmity in Ireland, in the Middle East, in Central America, at the negotiation tables of every nation, and in our prisons and homes.

Are the peacemakers blessed? They are the sons and daughters of God. As Christians our job is, first of all, to pray for peace. We need to pray with no illusions—with eyes wide open, knowing that, apart from God, real peace between natural enemies is an impossibility. We have a responsibility to pray without ceasing for the peacemakers, whoever they are and wherever they are. But, even more pertinent, we must ask God to make us peacemakers day by day in our own lives and circles of influence, wherever we are. Blessed, indeed, are the peacemakers.

12

Dangerous Dialog

What image comes to mind when you hear the word *prayer?* Is prayer a process by which we invoke a protecting God, one who keeps us under his wings, and therefore free from harm? That's the God of the writer of Psalm 121: "The Lord watches over you—the Lord is your shade at your right hand; the sun will not harm you by day, nor the moon by night. The Lord will keep you from all harm—he will watch over your life; the Lord will watch over your coming and going . . . " (vv. 5-8). These kinds of prayers, offered to keep us from all evil, are and have been uttered as far back as Abraham. But there is also a danger in them. We can begin to see them as some sort of voodoo chant to keep evil spirits away. I recently came across an anonymous poem that epitomizes that kind of theology, and I admit that the poetry is as bad as the theology:

> A father was holding a son in his arms,
> A loud barking dog was near.
> He knew his father would keep him from harm,

And so he did not feel any fear.
When his father put him down and set him upon a large log,
He gazed at his father from down on the ground,
And said, "Please, father, now pick up the dog."

Perhaps our most sincere or, if you will, existential prayers are those born in the terror of the moment when we implore God to pick us up and hold us, or to remove the danger. We can remember times when God has done exactly that. We have a sound biblical basis to believe in that kind of prayer. God *did* deliver Abraham, Jacob, Joseph, David, Peter, Paul, and Silas, to name just a few. But that "safe harbor" sort of prayer, "Oh, Lord, I'm in trouble! Help!" is just part of the total prayer picture. I would hope that another image that comes to mind as we think about prayer is that of a launching pad.

When you begin to pray, your life can take on all kinds of perils and problems that you never had before. Think about it. As far as we know, Abraham was living a comfortable, trouble-free life until he began to pray. It was through prayer that he heard God's message to leave home, move out, hit the road for an unknown destination, and start a journey of indeterminate length. His life became exceedingly difficult and dangerous. Yes, he had the protective safety of God's love, but his life was much more complicated.

Prayer was the launching pad for Moses as well. He was quietly tending sheep in the Midian hills, leading a settled life with his wife and sons and his father-in-law. Things changed when he started to pray. It started dramatically enough at a burning bush, where he heard God speak to him and entrust him with an impossible task—that of leading the Israelites out of Egypt. From one perspective, that was the last really comfortable day of Moses' life until his death on Mount Nebo. At every step of the way over the next 40 years he had major problems.

As far as we know, Jesus' mother Mary had no more problems than the average teenage girl in Nazareth. That fateful day when God spoke to her changed all that. She suffered misunderstanding, hardship, exile, and, ultimately, witnessed the untimely and cruel death of her firstborn son. Life became exceedingly difficult.

Peter, James, John, and Andrew were comfortable, middle-class businessmen, settled and respected in their community, until their dialog with Jesus began. As they responded to his invitation to, "Follow me," all of that ended. They embarked on three years of intense ministry and then carried out the commission to "go and make disciples of all nations" (Matt. 28:19) in the face of unimaginable adversity and persecution. The peaceful fishermen's lives at Galilee were gone forever.

That is the peril of prayer. Our prayers may begin with pleas for peace and prosperity and protection, but, as we begin to talk to God and hear him speak to us, life may never be the same. It may become, as it did in all the cases we mentioned here, very difficult.

I'm especially fond of the story Matthew tells in Chapter 14 of his gospel, and it's one that has a good deal to teach us about this matter of prayer. The disciples had put to sea without Jesus, and a storm had arisen. These veteran sailors and fishermen were crossing the lake in a boat. What could be more simple? It was a lake they knew well, and a fairly small one. The majority of the disciples were trained and equipped for just that sort of thing. They knew all about boats, lakes, wind, and water. It was a piece of cake. They were crossing the lake with self-assurance, confident of handling any and all problems, and not even thinking about prayer.

It's a familiar script for most of us. We row our boat across life's lake confident in our own abilities. We know how to do our job, handle our marriage, deal with our kids, and invest our money. Who needs prayer for that? Prayer is for big emergencies. That's why it's so distressing when in the ordinary, everyday areas where we are competent, life caves in. We think we have done such a super job of parenting, and then a call from the principal's office or the police station rocks that nice, comfortable boat. Your business may have been running smoothly, expanding and making money, when the unforeseen happens—falling oil prices or an unreliable partner—and your boat starts taking on water. In the very midst of the ordinary and routine, things can suddenly get out of hand, just as they did for those sailors and fishermen.

How reassuring it is to read that Jesus came to them walking on the water, even before they cried out. That's the incredible fact of prayer. Before we ask, before we're even aware of the danger, God is meeting us. He initiates the dialog, as Jesus did in this incident. "Take courage! It is I. Don't be afraid" (Matt. 14:27). Matthew tells us that when they saw him they were terrified. The solution to their life-threatening situation loomed on the horizon, and they were afraid, certain they were seeing a ghost. Most of us can identify with that. Sometimes when God intervenes dramatically in answer to our needs, we're just as incredulous.

One day over lunch a parishioner who was a new Christian was telling me about an experience he had had. His business had been facing financial ruin when he got what he thought was a clear message from God about a course of action. It seemed unlikely, even bizarre, and he had a hard time believing God had prompted him. But, he said, "I did it. I look back now and I realize that was the turning point in my business difficulties."

Even at the sound of Jesus' voice, the disciples were not entirely convinced that this apparition was, in fact, their Lord—or at least we know that Peter was not. Dear, impetuous Peter set up a test: "Lord, if it's you . . . tell me to come to you on the water." Can you imagine the scene? The boat was rocking crazily, the waves were enormous, and the wind was howling. Yet Peter had faith enough to step out of the boat when Jesus said, "Come." To me that's a piercing analogy of what prayer is. Yes, Jesus comes to us in the midst of disasters, calamities, and problems, but he bids us to "come," to step out of the boat, to make a faith commitment, to act on the directions he gives us.

Peter did that. He stood up, climbed over the rail, and actually walked on the water. Peter did the impossible. Of all people, Peter was well aware that you cannot walk on water. He had spent all his years on the water, seining for bait, sailing boats, catching fish. But, convinced he could do it and with his eyes on Jesus, he attempted the impossible—and succeeded for a time.

It's a miracle, and some of us have lived long enough to see at least a few of those. Many people who are in the medical profession have seen things that defy explanation. There are cures and healings and remissions that shouldn't happen and couldn't happen, and they can only be attributed to the prayers of the many, faithful believers who are claiming miracles. Peter's attempt to do the impossible was not prompted by courage but by faith. When the Lord asks *us* to climb over the rail of that boat, to plunge into what seems like certain danger, we do it by faith. Peter's was all too short-lived. Full of faith and walking on the water, Peter became aware of his impossible situation and promptly began to sink. He cried out, "Lord, save me!" Jesus caught him immediately, but with a reproof: "You of little faith . . . why did you doubt?" (v. 31).

An economist was presenting a lecture in downtown Seattle a while back. She began by tacking up a large piece of paper on a board in the front of the room. Next she took a crayon and put a heavy, black dot in the middle of the paper. "What do you see?" she asked. The response was unanimous, "A black dot." She pointed out that not a single person mentioned the white paper. All saw only the black dot. We might say that when Peter had his eyes on the sheet of white paper, he was able to do the miraculous. As soon as he saw the black dot, he began to sink.

Authentic prayer may lead us into peril or difficulty. It may get us out of the boat, attempting to walk on the water. A good many of my parishioners seem to be doing that. Ann Lund is a young nurse, slight and frail, and she spend three months serving at a medical station in Ethiopia at the height of the famine disaster of 1985. She was able to "walk on the water" in the midst of that horrendous situation because she saw more than the black dot of famine. She saw the larger landscape of God's plans and purposes.

For some time now, another parishioner, Chester Biesen, three-score years and plus, has been a lay missionary to India for part of every year. He preaches in the bush, foregoing toilet facilities, eating strange foods, enduring all kinds of rugged conditions. His overall goal is to evangelize India, but his most immediate one on his last trip was to build a home for battered wives. Chet's prayers often launch him into hardship and long hours. However, in the midst of it all, he seems to be walking on the water.

Two women, Gloria Cole and Margaret Larson, have heard God's clear guidance to do something about hunger. They have just passed the million mark in the number of sandwiches that they have made and distributed to the street people of our city. Those neighborhoods are dangerous, and they could be mugged or killed. They go anyway. They have been called to get out of the boat.

I love the story of the old gentleman who was still playing golf, though his eyes had failed to the extent that he could hardly tell the caddy from the golf cart. He was an expert putter and was often asked how he could still do that so well. "It's very simple," he said. "When I putt I tip my bifocals somewhat. In that position, I see two balls, one large and one small, and two cups, one large and one small. All I have to do is hit the small ball into the large cup." I suggest that with Jesus' help, we can tip our spectacles and look with the eyes of faith. We can begin to perceive that the problems and difficulties are small compared to the vast resources of a mighty God.

Prayer is basically dialog. God meets us in that dialog. He was waiting for us before we knew our need, as he was with those fishermen on the stormy lake. That dialog is the means of comfort, protection, and deliverance, but it is also the springboard for the adventure of faith. As we pray for the hurts of our family, friends, and world, God calls us to be an answer to those prayers.

That's the experience of a friend of ours from Baltimore. She spent some time with us last year and told us this unusual story about her trip. She changed planes in Chicago and was waiting for her flight to Seattle when she noticed a woman with a baby. The infant was screaming relentlessly. What do you do as a Christian when you're sitting in the airport next to a woman with a frantic baby? You're concerned, of course, but you're probably hoping you won't get the seat next to that baby on the plane. Normie was concerned, and she started praying, asking the Lord to bless the mother and quiet the child. The baby kept crying. Our friend felt God directing her to go over and offer help, which she did. The mother was eager to talk about her unhappy situation. "As I left the house this morning, I was in such a hurry that I left the baby's bottles on the kitchen counter. My little girl is so hungry, and I have nothing to feed her."

Normie did more than sympathize. She resolved to go and find that baby a bottle. She had 55 minutes until plane time. The first thing she did was inquire about the location of the nearest drugstore. There was one in the bottom of the Hilton Hotel, about a 20-minute walk away. If she hurried, she'd have just enough time. However, when she arrived at the drugstore, she was told they were all out of bottles. The last one had just been sold. She was a little chagrined, but continued to pray. "Lord, now what will I do?" At that very moment, a woman went by pushing a baby in a stroller. Normie took out after her and recounted the plight of the mother and baby. The woman was all sympathy. "I've got two bottles with me," she said, "you can have this one."

Triumphantly, Normie rushed back to the gate with 15 minutes to spare. The mother and the baby had disappeared. Told that a second plane was leaving for Seattle at another gate, she immediately ran over there, found the flight attendant, and told her the story. "There's a mother and screaming baby on your plane. Will you give her this bottle and some milk? I know you'll be glad you did." With a great sense of accomplishment, Normie returned to her gate and boarded her plane. Lo and behold, a few seats away were the mother and the baby. They had been seated first, the usual procedure for passengers with small children.

A lesser woman would have given up in defeat. Not Normie. She prayed again "Lord, now what do I do?" With five minutes to go before departure, she rushed up to tell the flight attendant about the problem. "Listen, it'll be better for all of us if you do what I tell you. Get on the radio and call that other plane leaving for Seattle. That flight attendant is holding a milk bottle, and there is no baby on that flight. Have her bring it over here." Just as the plane was leaving, the milk bottle arrived. Normie delivered it to the mother personally. That grateful woman, with no inkling of the 55-minute drama, simply said, "Oh, thank you."

That whole, wild adventure began with a prayer of concern, but our friend's unyielding determination to be a part of God's answer to that prayer made it happen. The peril of prayer is that you and I will make our prayer life the means to ensure a safe harbor. If you spend the rest of your life being protected, kept, comforted, held, and shielded, you will miss God's best for you. We're being asked to climb over the rail and walk on the water.

Paul's prayers led him to Asia Minor and rejection. They led him to Macedonia and the consequent beatings and stonings. They led him to Jerusalem and prison, to Rome and, as far as we know, to death. Paul's prayers did not produce a comfortable life. Yes, the Comforter was with him in all of the adversities, but his life was as thorny and unpredictable as ours is meant to be.

You may have read about the famous radio message delivered by Chesty Puller, a Marine general in the Korean War: ". . . we've got the enemy on our right flank, our left flank, in front of us, and behind us. They won't get away this time." You might say he had the ability to focus on the white paper and ignore the black dot.

When Mother Teresa received her honorary degree from Georgetown University in 1982, she said, "Don't be afraid. God loves you. You are precious to him. He says, 'I called you by your name. You are mine. Water cannot drown you. Fire will not burn you. I will give up nations for you. You are precious to me. I love you.'" That is what we hear God saying to us in prayer. With that assurance, we can tackle the biggest challenge he sends our way—a baby needing a bottle at O'Hare Airport, or an Ethiopian famine. As we climb over the rail and walk on the water, we discover that God's resources are all-sufficient.

If you have yet to hear God's call to holy living, you may hear it in the dialog of prayer. If you are living out that call, prayer will not only nourish and sustain you, but provide the impetus to be God's person, doing God's work in the world. The holy life is the life of prayer and, conversely, prayer is the lifeline of the holy life. It is the means by which we know God and his will for us. It is a means by which we can affect the lives of our friends and neighbors and perhaps even change the world.

Other Christian Growth Books:

The Faith-Hardy Christian by Gary L. Harbaugh
Criticizing by William J. Diehm
The Power of Affirming Touch by Wilson Wayne Grant
Celebrating God's Presence by William E. Hulme
Dealing with Your Discontent by Peter L. Steinke